# MIME MINISTRY

An illustrated, easy-to-follow
guidebook for organizing,
programming and training
a troupe of Christian mimes

## SUSIE KELLY TOOMEY

**Meriwether Publishing Ltd.**
Colorado Springs, Colorado

**Meriwether Publishing Ltd., Publisher**
**P.O. Box 7710**
**Colorado Springs, CO 80933**

**Executive Editor: Arthur Zapel**
**Manuscript Editor: Kathy Pijanowski**
**Designer: Michelle Z. Gallardo**
**Photographer: Ted Zapel**

**The Library of Congress has cataloged the first
printing of this title as follows:**

Toomey, Susie Kelly
    Mime ministry : an illustrated, easy-to-follow
guidebook for organizing, programming, and training a troupe of Christian mimes / by Susie Kelly
Toomey. — 1st ed. — Colorado Springs, Colo. :
Meriwether Pub., c1986.

    167 p. : ill. ; 22 cm.

    Bibliography: p. 163-167.
    IBSN 0-916260-37-2 (pbk.)

    1. Drama in Christian education. 2. Mime—Study
and teaching. I. Title.
BV1534.4T66    1986    246'.7—dc19    85-63774
                              AACR 2 MARC

Library of Congress

*This book is lovingly dedicated to*
*Rick, Kelly and Chris.*


## Acknowledgements

I wish to express my sincere appreciation
to the following people for their encouragement
and help in the preparation of this book:

my husband, for his ongoing
encouragement, ideas and practical help

members of my mime troupe for trying out
my skits and making them real

Tonda Strong, for allowing me the use
of her poem

the Gaither and Benson Music Companies

Sam Kelly, for his photographic work

and my publisher, for providing me with
the opportunity to share my ideas
and ministry

# EDITOR'S NOTE TO READER

*We ventured to publish this first mime ministry handbook because we believe that this activity, along with clown ministry, offers a unique expression of Christian celebration and outreach.*

*It is our hope that future editions of this book will be as current and supportive as we have endeavored to make this first edition. So that we may achieve this goal, we ask that you write us about your ideas and provide us reports of your mime ministry events. With your permission, we would like to share your experiences with others to help inspire the growth of other mime ministry groups.*

*Thank you in advance for your interest and participation in making this the best possible workbook for training mime ministers.*

# TABLE OF CONTENTS

*Our thanks to the mime models featured
in this book:*

**Jeff Stone**, entertainer and conceptual theatrician,
of Colorado Springs, Colorado

**The Reverend Steve Harrington**,
Minister of Young Adults,
and **Nancy Harrington**, both of First Presbyterian Church
of Colorado Springs, Colorado

# INTRODUCTION

Pantomime seems to set free the inner world of one's imagination and creativity, just as metamorphasis sets a beautiful butterfly into glorious flight from its cocoon.

*Mime* is the expression or communication of an emotion, a thought, an idea or a story through body gestures and facial expressions, and without any spoken words.

*A mime* is the communicator of these gestures and facial expressions.

Mime has been used in dramatic presentations and by circus clowns for centuries, and is now finding its way into the church. Many books have been written on the history and techniques of mime as an art, but little information is available for incorporating mime into the church.

Mime can contribute to Christian ministry in a powerful way. I hope that this book will excite you about the possibilities of using mime in the church, and that it will be a valuable tool as you endeavor to share the gospel of Jesus Christ through mime.

— *Susie Kelly Toomey*

# CHAPTER 1:

# MIME —
# YESTERDAY
# & TODAY

**M**ime is as ancient as humankind. From the earliest times, people communicated through gestures and by acting out what they wanted or needed. Primitive cultures practiced mime as a part of religious ceremonies, war dances, weather dances, harvest dances and dances before and after a hunt.

In time, however, mime gradually shifted from being simply a form of communication to being a popular form of entertainment. Mimed dramas focusing on the gods, myths and legends of great heroes became popular. Mime became a favorite part of the opera and enjoyed much success and growth under Emperor Augustus of Rome.

After the fall of the Roman empire, mime took on new themes, including those of morality and religion. The *commedia dell'arte*, an improvisational theatre form where actors played regular character roles in a variety of story situations, came into being as an outgrowth of other types of mime.

Several mimes have had a marked impact on the art of mime as we know it today. Jean Gaspard Batiste

---

*The word *he* is used generically throughout this book to denote all people, both male and female.

Debureau changed the scope of mime to include stories with plots and interaction among characters. Étienne Decroux introduced many exercises, illusions and techniques which contemporary mimes still use. Decroux became a much-sought-after teacher of mime, and many of his students became great performers in the theatre. Jean-Louis Barrault, a pupil of Decroux's, enjoyed his real success as a mime in "The Horseback Rider" and later in a film, *Les Enfants du Paradis,* in which he and Decroux performed together.

Certainly, one of the most well-known mimes the world over is the incomparable Marcel Marceau. Even people who have never heard of the word *mime* are at least familiar with one of its greatest artists. Those who study and perform mime today have studied Marceau's techniques, and for the most part, have imitated his style.

A few of the many other great mimes, from the days of the silent screen through today, are:

| | |
|---|---|
| *Charlie Chaplin* | *Emmett Kelly* |
| *Laurel and Hardy* | *Lucille Ball* |
| *Harpo Marx* | *Lou Jacobs* |
| *W.C. Fields* | *Dick Van Dyke* |
| *Red Skelton* | *Jerry Lewis* |
| *Carol Burnett* | *Sheilds and Yarnell* |

Mime has a rich history and an exciting future. Can mime in the church be a part of that future?

# CHAPTER 2

# RATIONALE FOR MIME IN CHRISTIAN MINISTRY

A nd God saw everything that he had made, and behold, it was very good." (Genesis 1:31a) So many visual images are pleasing to the eyes and have a significant impact on our lives. Just think about the thoughts and feelings you associate with a majestic mountain range, the colorful leaves of fall, awesome ocean waves on the seashore, a glorious sunrise, a peaceful mountain lake. Yes, God's creation is beautiful to behold, and most of us have experienced peace and joy while outdoors.

Just as seeing God's creation inspires positive feelings, other visual images influence us in significant ways. Someone could talk for an hour about the suffering caused by the starvation in Africa, and would probably not have the impact of one picture showing the deprived body of a starving child. We are moved by what we see.

Learning theory also teaches us that we retain much more of what we see than just what we hear. This concept means that if we are to effectively teach the things that God wants us to know, we need to use visual as well as verbal communication. To illustrate the importance of how we learn through sight, try to recall as many specific words spoken by others as you can, and then try to recall as many specific visual images from previous experiences as you can.

This chapter attempts to establish mime as a valid approach for communicating the gospel within the church and in other areas of Christian ministry. Mime is a visual form of communication that has not been used to a great extent within the church, although the use of visual images has a long religious history. The use of the cross, the Lord's Supper and baptism are excellent examples of visual symbolism. It is hoped that this chapter will create some excitement about how the art form of mime can be used to help Christians share the message of Jesus Christ in a creative and effective way.

Unfortunately, we Christians have come to rely on words as our primary, and at times our only, means of communicating. Some great preachers like Jonathan Edwards were masters at creating visual images with words. If you have ever read his sermon entitled "Sinners in the Hands of an Angry God," you probably experienced a little fear as you imagined dangling over the pit of hell like a spider dangling from a single strand of its web. Few people, however, possess the speaking ability to create these vivid pictures. Therefore, we need to use visual images more often to be really effective communicators.

God uses visual images to communicate things which are at the very foundation of our faith. Is your understanding of faith enhanced by the portrait of Noah building the ark? Can you fully comprehend obedience unless you visualize Abraham holding a knife over his son Isaac? Does God's power not take on greater meaning as you picture Moses holding his rod out as the Red Sea parts? Isn't the power of prayer more real to you when you see, in your mind, Daniel amidst the lions? Doesn't God's protection of us mean more when you imagine David standing over the body of Goliath?

Jesus was the master teacher, and he relied heavily on visual images to communicate his message. Christ used parables to convey the true meaning of the gospel. These parables were more visual stories than elaborate dialogue. Many parables begin with the phrase *like unto,* which means that some visual scenes will be used to help us better understand something. To illustrate, let's take a look at a few images developed in the parables:

- seed growing only when the sower plants it in good soil (Mark 4:1-8)
- the humility of the publican as he prays with head bowed while the Pharisee boastfully looks toward heaven (Luke 18:10-14)
- a rich man lifting up his eyes from the torment of hell while the beggar Lazarus resides in heaven with Abraham (Luke 16:19-31)
- a priest and another religious leader passing by a half-dead man before a compassionate Samaritan man stops to help the wounded man (Luke 10:30-37)
- a father running to meet his son, who has returned from a far country, and celebrating by killing a fatted calf (Luke 15:11-32)

The teachings of Jesus are profound and certainly enhance our knowledge of him. However, the words of Jesus that were recorded in the Bible could be placed in a pamphlet. Our understanding of Christ probably is influenced in a greater way by what he did than what he said. Jesus acted out the gospel in a beautiful way. Let's look at a few brief scenes as examples:

- Jesus sitting with the scribes in the temple and preparing to be about his Father's business
- Jesus being baptized by John and affirmed as God's Son by God's spirit descending upon him like a dove
- Jesus exhibiting his power by calming the angry sea
- Jesus showing tenderness by taking time for the children

- Jesus giving a picture of the meaning of forgiveness by bending to write in the sand rather than condemn the adulterous woman
- Jesus providing a glimpse of what real humility is by washing the disciples' feet
- Jesus giving a view of brotherly love through the tears he shed for his friend Lazarus
- Jesus helping us to see what acceptance of others is all about by having dinner with an unpopular tax collector named Lazarus
- Jesus providing the ultimate image of sacrificial love by giving his life on a cross

Yes, it's true that one picture is worth a thousand words; and aren't you thankful for the numerous pictures of Jesus Christ that are painted in scripture?

One reason the Bible contains so many visual images is because many principles of our faith are difficult to explain in words. As an example, think how difficult it is to define faith. However, faith can be vividly illustrated through a series of actions. If you want to better understand what faith is, close your eyes and ask a friend to lead you around your house without letting you bump into something. If you have never done this, you will learn a little something about faith. Mime is a beautiful vehicle for enriching our understanding of the Christian faith.

Renowned Christian mime Randall Bane has this to say about mimes representing our faith:

*Participants in church pantomime have a different responsibility from those using the form in other situations. Unless the event is a purely social or cultural gathering held in a church building, the pantomime presentation should be consciously seen as a ministry. If the pantomime is to be a worship piece* *(perhaps replacing a choir number or used as a response to the reading of the gospel), then those who perform it are expressing to God the praise of the worshippers. Therefore, the performer should responsibly represent the faith of those believers. If the pantomime piece is to teach or edify those present, the powerful and memorable images with which the performer illustrates the truths of the gospel may sink deep and last long. Here the performer bears responsibility to God for the integrity with which his word is expressed. Certainly the production of a pantomime should be a joyful experience but, as with all service to God and his church, this effort should be entered into with a sense of reverence for the content to be presented and an awareness of the potential power of this art form. Some of the performing arts have been totally out of favor with the church because the Good News became less important than the newspaper or because the star of the production took all the glory for himself, denying the glory to the Savior. It is good to remember that the whiteface make-up does not hide what is going on inside. It makes it clearer!\**

Let's summarize the rationale that has been discussed for using mime in Christian ministry:

- Learning theory tells us that we remember things that we see more than things we just hear.
- The Bible contains countless visual images to help in our understanding of God.
- Jesus relied heavily on actions and visual stories to communicate the gospel.

*From *The Art of Pantomime in the Church,* filmstrip with Randall Bane (Colorado Springs, CO: Meriwether Publishing Ltd., 1982), p. 1 of reference script.

- Spiritual truths and principles are sometimes easier to portray through visual images than through words.

A commonly used expression is *I see.* When we use this phrase, we mean *I perceive, I understand, I know* or *I comprehend.* When someone sees a mimed explanation of a spiritual truth, they will be helped to perceive, understand, know and comprehend. Using mime in Christian ministry makes sense. In addition, it is entertaining and will possibly attract the attention of some people who would not listen to a sermon or a verbal witness about Christ. Now that we've established a rationale for using mime in Christian ministry, let's learn how to do it!

CHAPTER 3:

# PURPOSE OF A CHRISTIAN MIME MINISTRY

T he purpose of a Christian mime ministry is to share the love and gospel of Jesus Christ in a unique and creative way. Sometimes the surface purpose is entertainment, sometimes communication, sometimes worship — but the overall purpose is always to give glory to God. In Matthew 28:19-20, we are told to go and teach the world about Jesus Christ. Just as puppet teams, drama troupes and musical ensembles have been used to communicate God's love, mime can also be used effectively to share the gospel. Reasons for mime's effectiveness include the following:

- **Mimes and clown mimes are instant attention-getters** because of their make-up and outward appearance. Once a mime has people's attention, he can present the gospel.

There is a mime who performs at Sea World as people come into one of the outdoor theatres. Although hundreds of people are filing into the theatre over an hour's time, the mime is able to hold the audience's attention.

- **Mimes can communicate feelings and thoughts in a unique way.** It is a fact that we retain much more of what we see than what we simply hear. Combine the

seeing with the quality of uniqueness, and you have a super method of communication. To go a step further, it is a fact that we retain more of what we experience than what we only hear and see. In many instances, a mime is touching and visually expressing feelings, thoughts and emotions that his audience is experiencing. This unified experience can make a significant impact on the spectators' hearts and lives.

- **Mimes can present important lessons and messages in a humorous way.** I have sat through a few thousand sermons in my lifetime — some great, some not so good. I must (shamefully) admit that even though I may forget the words of the sermon, I can usually remember a humorous anecdote or a touching illustration. As I reflect on, and sometimes retell, the anecdote, I can usually call to mind the meat of the sermon.

  A mime can plant this same type of seed, a seed that, as it is fertilized and nurtured, will grow and mature, and perhaps bring a heart closer — if only a little — to God.

- **The actor himself becomes anonymous: the attention is focused on the character and message of the mime.** For centuries, people have hidden behind masks. Trick-or-treaters put on horror and character masks and often take on a whole new personality. Thieves put on bandanas and ski masks to conceal their identity, and often end up doing things that they would never do if their faces were visible.

  There are many mimes who would never feel comfortable performing in front of people if they were not hidden by a clown face or a mime face. But when the mask is on, they find a release of their fears or inhibitions and take on a new personality as they physically express what they otherwise could not say.

  Sometimes the mime face also makes it easier for the audience to see the message if the mime is separated from the personality of the person.

Yes, mime does have a place in Christian ministry — a very effective place!

CHAPTER 4:

# HOW TO ORGANIZE A MIME TROUPE

A mime troupe can develop from just one interested person. This person should first seek some understanding of the purpose and possibilities of such a ministry.

Next, other interested people should be recruited and enlisted. I began the troupe in my present church by enlisting several youth to present a mime routine for the youth group during youth week. Following the mime routine (for which the actors donned costumes and make-up), I shared with the youth group the possibilities of a drama group using mime.

We then had a one-month enlistment period. For your church, I suggest that new people not be allowed to join the group after a one-month sign-up period except at designated times — perhaps every three to four months. This schedule prevents constant repetition of teaching mime techniques, make-up application, etc. This waiting period also allows people time to consider whether or not they really want to become a part of this particular ministry.

After the first enlistment period, our troupe was organized. We gave our group a name — The Rainbow Connection — and we use as our theme song the song from

*The Muppet Movie* entitled "The Rainbow Connection." The group had a great time choosing the name, designing the logo, etc.

At the first meeting, the group should discuss the opportunities of this new ministry and set up some goals. It should be continually emphasized that this group's purpose is ministry, and not merely appearing at parties and festivals to entertain.

Some goals your group could set are:

- first and foremost, to glorify God in all that we do
- to serve as ministers of the gospel through the creative expression of mime
- to reach out to people, both within and outside of the church, sharing the message of hope and love of Jesus Christ

Once your group has established its goals and priorities, members should set up a weekly or bi-weekly time to meet, decide on a meeting place, etc.

Your mime troupe will have to study many different techniques and aspects of mime before it can begin its ministry. It is important that each mime has enough basics, enough practice time and enough self-confidence before he is asked to take that step into the watchful world of onlookers.

# CHAPTER 5:

# PROGRAMMING A MIME MINISTRY

**W**hat types of things can a mime troupe do? Where can a mime troupe go to minister? Can ministry take place inside and outside the church? The answers to these questions will vary with each group. The first step in programming your ministry would be to brainstorm all the possibilities for ministry in your area. Some groups will have opportunities that others will not.

Possibilities include performances at a children's home, a campground, a state park, a prison, your church. Some groups might be located in a town where a lot of tourists visit; some in an inner-city situation where streets and local parks would provide great opportunities for ministry. Just take a look at your surroundings. Talk with your local chamber of commerce or visitor's bureau.

Below is a list of ideas to get you started:

- *children's homes*
- *housing projects*
- *parades*
- *school assemblies*
- *shopping malls*
- *libraries*
- *nursing homes*
- *senior citizen homes*
- *school talent shows*
- *city and state parks and playgrounds*
- *campgrounds*

- *church parties and banquets*
- *civic group meetings*
- *children's churches*
- *promotions*
- *programs for the deaf*
- *prisons and jails*
- *programs for mentally retarded and handicapped children (schools, camps)*
- *mission trips*
- *summer camps (YMCA, 4-H, church, scout)*
- *worship services*
- *vacation Bible school*
- *festivals, parties*
- *church fellowships*
- *street corners*
- *hospitals*

Mime performers and ministers will be warmly welcomed in most of the places listed above. In some instances, however, public schools will not allow mime ministry sketches to be performed if the message is overtly religious or obviously represents any specific faith. The principle of separation of church and state must be respected in schools and other public institutions. Another area where resistance might be met is in presentations during worship services. While some churches will readily accept this type of creative dramatic presentation, other churches will be more hesitant and restrictive.

If you are really interested in performing during the worship times, but find the pastor or congregation hesitant, try to work with them in a positive way. Sometimes people are apprehensive because they do not fully understand your purpose and your ministry. Begin by talking with your church staff and other individuals and share with them how you feel your ministry might fit into the worship time. Invite them to preview one of your mime sketches. If they still do not approve, be positive, patient and prayerful. Find out whether they disapprove of your message or the way (mime) you are presenting the message. In time, your church members might change their minds — or they may not. But remember that there are plenty more opportunities outside the church where you can have a very effective ministry!

Below is a poem written by a friend following a mime presentation during a Sunday morning worship service. I hope this poem* will be an encouragement to you, as it was to me.

## Sunday Morning Clowns

*The clowns came to worship service today.*
*Some folks shook their heads*
*In dismay.*
*I even heard one woman say:*
*"It's a shame!*
*Brings dishonor to His name!"*

*Each clown knew his memorized part.*
*Folks couldn't see*
*The silent clown's heart.*
*But God saw it was better*
*Than a hardened heart.*
*It's a shame.*
*Cold hearts dishonor His name.*

*Some folks are too shy to speak without a mask.*
*But they can serve our Lord*
*Through this kind of task.*
*Of our attitudes and thoughts,*
*We must ask:*
*"Who are the real clowns, anyway?"*
*We who are fools*
*By the things we say!*

*Clowns can contribute to worship in their*
*    own special way.*
*Surely there's room here*
*For those dear clowns today.*
*I need only stop and pray:*
*"Lord, send in the clowns*
*And turn my heart around."*

*The clowns have taught us without a sound.*
*They've turned inner self upside-down.*
*Who tries to change a sour frown?*
*Who understands better*

---

*Poem by Tonda Strong (1985). Used by permission.

*When things go wrong*
*Than these clowns*
*Who've brought to me a new song?*

*(Lord, an encourager only*
*I want to be —*
*to our Rainbow Connection Ministry!)*

**— Tonda Strong**

Now that you have an idea of *where* to go, *what* can you do when you get there? The possibilities can be grouped into the following categories:

- skits with a biblical message
- skits with a value lesson
- skits done just for fun
- musical and scriptural interpretations
- promotions
- walk-arounds

What you do in the area of mime depends upon your training as a mime and your natural talent. Mime skits, promotional sketches and musical and scriptural interpretations can be taught to most people with a normal amount of body coordination. Some walk-arounds can be taught, but much of this type of mime comes as a creative expression of one's inner thoughts, humor and feelings.

Let's look at the categories:

## Skits and Interpretations

Skits and interpretations with a Christian message can be presented in a variety of settings. Some of these skits can often be used to teach values, where Christian teachings are inappropriate. For example, a local school board might not allow skits teaching biblical truths in a classroom or school assembly, but would allow mime skits teaching values such as honesty, love and obedience to one's parents.

Many times skits can be done as attention-getters; that is, a humorous mime sketch with no teaching purpose is performed for the pure enjoyment of onlookers.

Once you have the audience's attention, you can present your skit with a message.

# Promotion

Being in a parade does not present a real opportunity for Christian ministry, but it does provide an opportunity for greater visibility within your community. Although the best publicity for your group is word of mouth, other opportunities should not be overlooked. For example, my clown troupe led a workshop on clowning two years ago during Funfest, a week-long community festival. The local newspaper did a story on our group. A year and a half later, the newspaper asked to do a full-page follow-up story entitled "Clowning For Christ's Sake." Wow! We began getting invitations from groups up to 100 miles away. Since we were offered more opportunities than we could accept, I referred many inquirers to other clown troupes in our area.

Your local newspaper may not come to you, but it sure wouldn't hurt to contact its editors. Most feature writers are always looking for something unique to profile.

Mime is also an effective means of promoting special events and making various announcements. Advertising management consultants will verify the fact that an effective ad campaign is worth its weight in gold. In the same way, the creative use of mime can turn the otherwise dull promotion of activities and events into an interesting and enjoyable time for all concerned, as well as probably boost attendance.

# Walk-Arounds

*Walk-arounds* is the name I give to spontaneous performances. Many opportunities for this type of mime are available. For instance, visiting from room to room in a nursing home or hospital offers the mime a chance to be creative and spontaneous while adding a little spark to the patients' lives. A mime will always have an audience by walking around at festivals, fellowships, parks, playgrounds, campgrounds, shopping malls, etc., and simply reacting to various people.

My family and I have visited Sea World, both in California and Florida. For several of the shows, it is necessary to arrive at the outdoor theatres early in order to get a good seat. The heat and sunlight, coupled with the long wait, could make for an unpleasant experience. But Sea World is on its toes! Audiences are pleasantly entertained by a mime who greets his guests in creative, humorous ways, often performing take-offs on the guests themselves. For example, he might get behind someone and mimic the way that person is walking. Or he might find a couple walking in, and after stepping in front of the man, he might put his hand on the woman's shoulder and walk with her; her reaction is usually hilarious when she discovers the hand belongs to the mime. As the audience is totally engrossed in the mime's every move, time slips away ever so quickly!

Opportunities are certainly out there just waiting to be seized. They are abundant for the diligent seeker.

# CHAPTER 6:

# MAKE-UP & COSTUMES

**M**imes were an important part of the theatre well before the invention of electric lights. Theatres were dimly lit with candles or lanterns, and it was extremely difficult to see facial expressions from a distance. Therefore, actors covered their faces with flour and outlined certain facial features with black charcoal.

Today, the white face remains a significant feature of a mime's character. The whiteface mask erases the individuality of the performer and allows him to explore and express his inner feelings.

Whiteface even has a religious significance. In most every race and culture, it is a symbol of death. The markings applied over the whiteface are symbols of new life. In Christianity, death of one's old self is necessary in order to gain new life in Christ. We read in 2 Corinthians 5:17, "Therefore if any man be in Christ, he is a new creature; old things are passed away; behold all things are become new."

Make-up on a mime is just like make-up on a woman — it can be neat and flattering, or it can be messy and unbecoming. The neatness of your make-up can speak by itself, so take much care in the application of your make-up.

# 2 Corinthians 5:17 (King James Version)

*Therefore if any man be in Christ,*

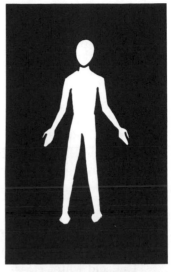

*he is a new creature;*

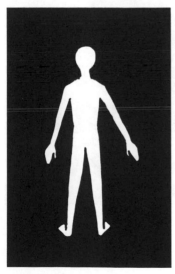

*old things are passsed away;*

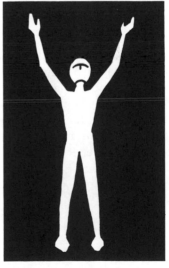

*behold, all things are become new.*

The items needed to apply whiteface include the following:

- baby oil
- clown white or white pancake make-up
- baby powder or cornstarch
- make-up sponge
- make-up brush
- black greasepaint or black eyeliner pencil
- red greasepaint (cream, sticks)
- tissues
- mirror
- towel, washcloth, soap
- spray bottle of water

## Application of Make-up

1. Wash your face and splash it with cold water. Pat it dry. (The cold water closes the pores.)
2. Pin your hair away from your face.

3. Look in the mirror and study your face. Study the muscles, contour and lines of your face. Do not try to hide your face, but rather, highlight your natural facial structure.

4. Apply a thin coat of baby oil all over your face. Then, using a tissue, gently pat your face, removing excess oil.

5. Using your fingers, apply clown white all over your face, including your eyelids and eyebrows. Take care to make a neat jawline. (Pancake make-up can be applied with a sponge.)

6. Pat your face repeatedly, using your fingers to give the face a smooth and even appearance.

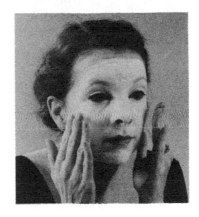

7. Using a tissue or cotton swab, wipe clean of clown white make-up your lips, eyebrows and any other areas to be colored.

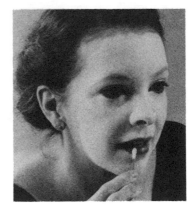

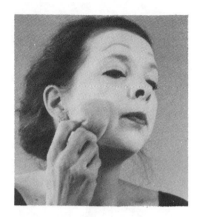

10. To set the clown white and make your face look dry and not sticky, tap your face lightly with a sock filled with powder or cornstarch.

11. Using a make-up brush or soft paintbrush, gently brush away excess powder or cornstarch from your face.

12. Apply red greasepaint to your lips. Outline using black pencil or grease-paint.

13. Paint your eyebrows and face markings and out-line your eyes using black pencil or greasepaint.

14. After your entire face has been made up, once again tap powder or cornstarch over your face.
15. Spray face lightly with water from a spray mist bottle.
16. To remove make-up, apply baby oil over entire face and wipe clean with a paper towel or tissue. Wash your face with soap and water.

Applying make-up is an art that takes some practice. If you make a mistake, simply wipe clean with baby oil and begin again.

The design of your face is up to you. It is OK to copy another mime's face for practice, but each mime should create a face that will be his trademark. It is probably best to first draft a design for your face on paper. Draw a face and then experiment with different markings. When designing your face, remember that too little is better than too much; too many markings will take away from the power of your facial expressions. All that is needed is something simple to outline your eyes and mouth, and perhaps a special something that is *you*. This special something could be a heart, a flower, a triangle, a cross, an initial, or perhaps a tear. Below are some examples of mime faces:

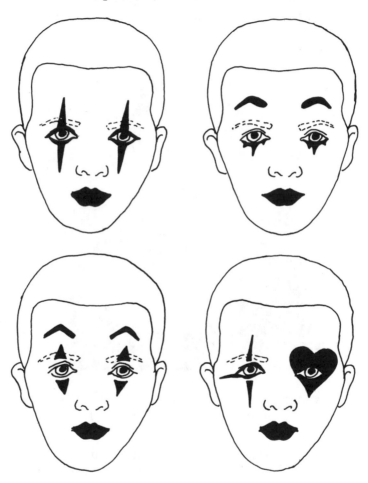

## PURCHASING MAKE-UP

Make-up can usually be purchased in stores which sell theatrical make-up, supplies and costumes, and in some magic shops. Make-up can also be ordered by mail from various companies (addresses listed in the back of this book under Resources). Check with the speech and drama teachers at your local high school or college to find out where they purchase such supplies locally.

# COSTUMES

The art of mime can be performed by actors in no costume or make-up, by clowns, and by mimes, dressed and made up as mimes in traditional mime make-up. There is no set costume for mimes, but the following suggestions might help you to determine what to wear:

- Your clothing should allow you freedom of movement.

- Your clothing is not your drawing card. Do not allow your choice of clothing to be a distraction from your purpose— communication.

- If you will be performing against a dark background, in dim lighting, etc., you might want to wear light-colored clothing and white gloves. If you will be performing in the bright daylight

or against a light background, darker clothing would be a better choice.

Mimes come in various sizes, shapes and costumes, so feel free to be yourself. I have seen many professional mimes wear leotards and tights, but this may not be as appropriate in Christian ministry. Personally, I like to wear something like painter's pants and a long-sleeved shirt, or all black (pants and shirt) or all white.

CHAPTER 7:

# WARM-UP
# EXERCISES
# & GAMES

The body is a mime's instrument, his tool. To perform at one's best, the body must be trained to meet the demands of the many gestures and movements. Warm-up is the first step. Just as an athlete performs warm-up exercises before an athletic contest or event, so must a mime prepare his body for physical performance.

The purpose of warm-up exercises is to loosen and gently stretch the various muscles of the body in preparation for more vigorous physical movements. Following is a descriptive list of warm-up exercises, although a variety of other exercises could be substituted.

# FACIAL EXERCISES

Practice these in front of a mirror if possible:

- Raise and lower the eyebrows eight to 10 times.

- Open the mouth wide and then close it. Repeat eight to 10 times.

- Keeping the lips closed, pull or rotate the lips to the left side and then to the right. Repeat several times.

- Draw your face inward. Shrivel your face like a prune. Relax. Repeat several times.

# BODY WARM-UPS

- **Arm Circles**
  Holding arms at the sides, at shoulder level and perpendicular to body, rotate arms forward in a circular motion for 30 seconds. Rotate arms backward for 30 seconds.

- **Waist Rotations**
  Stand erect. Bend forward for two counts, bend to the right side for two counts, bend backward for two counts, bend to the left side for two counts. Repeat several times.

- **Ankle Raises**
  Stand erect. Rise up on toes for four counts, then lower heels and stand flatfooted for four counts. Repeat several times.

- **Head Rotation**
  Stand erect. Rotate the head forward, then to the right side, then backward, then to the left side. Repeat. Reverse the rotation, going to the left side first. Repeat.

- **Leg Stretches**
  Begin on your hands and feet. Place the left foot about two feet in front of the right foot. Keeping the right foot flat on the floor, gently stretch the muscles in the back of the right leg. Hold for 10 seconds. Switch leg positions and repeat for the left leg.

# FUN WARM-UPS

1. **Warm-up:** *Face Passing*
   **Focus:** *imitation or mirror images; facial expresssions*

   Have participants sit in chairs or on the floor in a single-file line. The person at the back of the line is the leader. The leader taps the shoulder of the person in front of him, who turns around. The leader makes a facial gesture. That person, in turn, taps the shoulder of the person in front of him and passes on the facial gesture. This continues up the line. Different people can be the leader.

2. **Warm-up:** *Marionettes*
   **Focus:** *isolated body movements*

One person is the leader, and will verbally pull the strings of the marionettes. The marionettes must concentrate and visualize how a movement would look and then mime that image. The leader can use his own imagination to instruct the marionettes, but the following suggestions will get you started:

- Each marioncttc should begin with his body bent forward at the waist, arms and head hanging down.

- Say something like, "I am gently moving up and down the entire wooden frame to which your strings are attached." (The entire body should gently bounce and be very loose.)

- Say, "I am pulling up your head strings."

- Say, "I am pulling up your right shoulder strings."

- Say, "I am pulling up your right wrist strings," etc.

3. **Warm-up:** *Magic Clothing*
   **Focus:** *imagination; control of body movements*

Have participants scatter around the room, leaving plenty of room for movement. Ask them to react to and mime their reactions to the following situations:

- You find a magic glove. You put it on and it wants to float, as if filled with helium.

- You put on a magic pair of dancing shoes.

- You put on a magic hat that makes you sleepy. It keeps falling off, but you keep putting it back on.

Continue with other imaginative situations.

4. **Warm-up:** *Follow the Leader*
   **Focus:** *body control; isolated body movement; imitation and mirror images*

Have participants scatter, leaving plenty of room for movement. The leader should be in a position where everyone can see him. The leader makes various gestures and movements and the participants follow the leader by imitating his actions. Different people can be the leader.

Following the warm-up exercises with one or more of these fun warm-ups will add a bit of excitement and anticipation of what is yet to come. Encourage the participants to use their imaginations and enjoy these games.

# CHAPTER 8:

# TECHNIQUES OF MIME

There are many techniques of mime to be learned and practiced. Some logical sequence for learning these techniques should be followed, since many skills build on previously learned skills. With that thought in mind, the following sequence of mime techniques will be discussed:

- basic body position and body separations
- freeze positions
- slow-motion action
- mechanical people
- emotions
- simple tasks
- handling imaginary objects
- character impersonations
- animal impersonations
- mirror images
- illusions

# BASIC BODY POSITION AND BODY SEPARATIONS

In mime, the beginning body position from which all other movements evolve is called the *double-zero position*. Stand erect, heels together. Your chest is lifted without pulling your shoulders back. Your head is level, your arms and neck are relaxed. Your pelvis is tucked under, and your knees are straight.

In mime, one must learn to move each part of the body separately. There are five body separations: head, neck, chest, waist and pelvis. You should practice each one of these body movements over and over, watching yourself in a mirror whenever possible.

## A. Forward Inclinations:

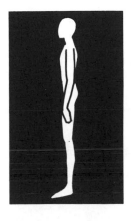

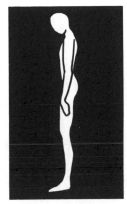

*Double-Zero*
*Position*

*Head*

*Neck*

*Chest*

*Waist*

*Pelvis*

# B. Rear Inclinations:

***Double-Zero
Position***

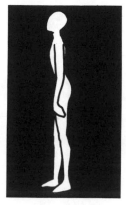

***Head***

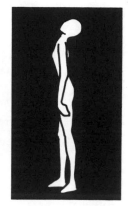

***Neck***

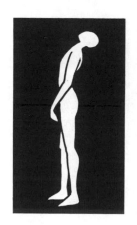

***Chest***

***Waist***

***Pelvis***

## C. Side Tilt:

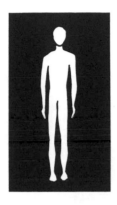

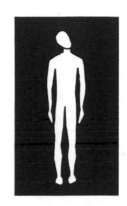

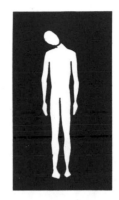

**Double-Zero Position**　　　**Head**　　　**Neck**

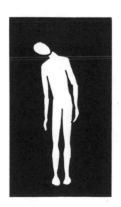

**Chest**　　　**Waist**　　　**Pelvis**

# FREEZE POSITIONS

After both practicing and watching others practice the body separations, you must then incorporate these separations into various combinations of body positions. One good practice method involves playing a game that many children play — Statues. The object of the game is to freeze, or become motionless in a particular position. To play the game, the leader should call out the positions listed below. Then after giving the actors an opportunity to react, the leader should shout out *freeze*. The actors freeze in their positions.

If there are several people participating, divide the group in half. Let one group watch as the other group plays the game. Allow the group watching to critique the body positions of the performing group. The groups should alternate performing and watching.

Below are some suggestions for statues:

- old man walking with a cane (Is the back slumped? Do the arms indicate support from the cane? Do the legs show weakness? etc.)
- a professional ballerina (Are the body separations precise, rigid, bold?)
- a butler (Does he have perfect posture? Does he appear to be very proper and dull?)
- a cowboy roping a steer (Does he look rugged, strong? Does his position indicate a freedom of movement in his arms?)
- a shy, timid child (Is his head dropped, shoulders slumped?)

# SLOW-MOTION ACTION

The next step in practicing body movement is to practice in slow motion. In this way, you must really understand, analyze and execute the movement in a manner which is realistic. Practice the following actions in slow motion:

- pitching a baseball
- painting a wall
- playing a piano
- chopping wood

It is important that, as a beginner in mime, you remember to break down your movements through this slow-motion technique before performing them.

# MECHANICAL PEOPLE

Perhaps one of the most recognized applications of mime in popular entertainment is that of the mechanical person or robot. Sheilds and Yarnell are two well-known mimes who brought the mechanical person to the public's attention. Even more recent is the dance craze — break dancing — in which dancers incorporate mechanical movements into their dance routines.

As a mechanical person, a mime must first be agile and have a good command of the body separations, as well as separations of the arms, legs and fingers. Next, a mime must assume and project an image of neutrality; that is, do not inject any personality or emotion into your character. Third, a mime must practice each detailed movement with a momentary stop or hesitation between movements. Movements are like staccato notes in music — quick, rigid, emphasized, separated.

The mechanical person can be fun for both the performer and the audience, but many hours of perfect practice are essential to the success of this type of mime. Researching books dealing in depth with the mechanical person would be helpful to the aspiring robot. (See Resources at the back of this book.)

# EMOTIONS

Training the body in physical techniques is only one aspect of mime. Learning to express character and emotions is another aspect.

The following exercise is a good beginning group exercise in learning to express emotions and attitudes through mime:

- Think up and write down on small sheets of paper as many emotions and attitudes as possible. Put these slips in a box.
- Going around the room, let each person take a turn drawing one of the papers from the box and expressing that emotion.
- Ask the group to guess what emotion the person is expressing.
- Ask the group to critique the person's expression. For instance, did they know, without a doubt, what the emotion was? What was really good about the gesture? What could be added or changed to make it better?
- Ask each person in the group to mime that same emotion. Encourage individuality and creativity, and remind the group of the points emphasized earlier about exaggeration, detail, sharpness, etc.

Below is a list of emotions, feelings and attitudes which could be used for this exercise:

| | |
|---|---|
| *happiness* | *fear* |
| *sadness* | *nervousness* |
| *disappointment* | *pride* |
| *shyness* | *heat* |
| *hatred* | *joy* |
| *silliness* | *intelligence* |
| *cold* | *excitement* |
| *wetness* | *pain* |
| *sleepiness* | *hesitation* |
| *grumpiness* | *love* |
| *laziness* | *boredom* |
| *sickness* | *mischievousness* |

Remember that we usually express emotions, feelings and attitudes with our entire bodies, not just with our faces. Remembering this will make a real difference in mime. For example, fear expressed only in the face is not nearly as realistic as fear expressed with the entire body. Look at the difference between these two pictures:

*The mime expresses fear using only facial expression.*

*Adding body gestures to the facial expression gives the viewer a much better understanding of the feeling the mime is trying to express.*

## SIMPLE TASKS

Once you feel comfortable expressing emotions and feelings, you should attempt to mime some simple tasks. You must remember to call upon the points already discussed, such as exaggeration, details, sharpness of

movements, etc. Try miming some of the following tasks and then add some of your own:

*sticky feet*
  *being tickled*
  *chewing bubblegum*
  *walking against a strong wind*
  *walking barefoot in the mud*
  *walking in deep snow*
  *sneezing*
  *crying*
  *yawning*
  *being seasick*
  *waking up*
  *having hiccups*

Try to always have someone watch and critique you; this feedback is extremely important.

## HANDLING IMAGINARY OBJECTS

A mime will often enact a scene involving the use of imaginary objects. He must give them substance and the illusion of reality. He must also remember how the object looks, how it feels, how it sounds, tastes and smells. He must then recreate the object as if it were real.

A mime must also use details in recreating objects, because only through details can the audience really understand what the mime wants to express. For example, if sharpening a pencil, don't simply stick a pencil in the sharpener, turn the handle, and walk away. Rather, after grinding the pencil, bring it out, look at it, put it back into the sharpener, grind it again, bring it out, look at it, and blow off the shavings.

Now, using your own creativity, mime the following situations:

*eat spaghetti*
*type on a typewriter*
*hold and pet a puppy*
*put on make-up*
*drive a car*
*pick an apple and eat it*
*open a door*
*lick an ice cream cone*
*sharpen a pencil*
*put on a coat and button it*
*jump a rope*
*cook pancakes*
*fly a kite*
*open a window*

There are some other important considerations in handling imaginary objects:

- **Weight of the object:** A mime should recreate the proper muscle tension needed in handling objects. For example, the act of picking up a bowling ball should create obvious muscle tension in the arms, hands and body, whereas picking up a pencil would not.

- **Size of the object:** Care should be taken to recreate the size of an object

accurately. For example, a basketball, a soccer ball and a beach ball are all different in size, as well as weight. Also, once in your hand, the size of the object must remain constant. For example, if you are holding an ice cream cone and you squeeze your hand smaller as time passes, you are essentially squeezing the cone. What a mess!

- **Approaching and taking the object:** When attempting to pick up an object, the mime must open his hands or arms larger than the object and then close in on the object. In this way, he is giving the illusion of actually picking up the object, rather than the object just suddenly appearing in his hand.
- **Releasing the object:** When you put an object down, be sure to let go of it. Place the object, relax your fingers and hand, open your hands to release it, and then move your hands away from it.

Now it is time for some hands-on experience. Form a circle and follow the sequence of steps below:

- The leader, holding an imaginary basketball, passes (hands, throws, bounces, etc.) the ball to another person in the circle.
- That person catches or takes the ball and passes it to another person.
- Continue passing until everyone has passed the ball a couple of times.
- Next, take a real basketball and pass it around the circle a couple of times. Ask each person to concentrate on the feel of the ball, the size, the weight, the releasing action, and the catching action.
- Put the real basketball aside and repeat the passing exercise with the imaginary ball.

- Now pass a heavy object around the circle, repeating the first five steps. This exercise should make each person more aware of the level of concentration and the attention to detail that is necessary in making a mimed action realistic and complete.
- Pass the following objects around the circle. Think about the points just discussed — the weight, the size, the shape, the texture, approaching, taking and releasing.

| | |
|---|---|
| *book* | *pencil* |
| *needle* | *large heavy suitcase* |
| *helium balloon on a* | *bag of groceries* |
| *string* | *barbell* |
| *glass of water* | *bowling ball* |
| *tall ladder* | *hot potato* |
| *handful of cooked* | |
| *spaghetti* | |

# CHARACTER IMPERSONATIONS

Character impersonation offers an opportunity for some real creativity. The mime must establish more than merely an occupation. A mime must give the character an identity, a personality, some depth.

Ask yourself the following questions:

- What type of actions might this character carry out?
- Does this character have any particular quirks or idiosyncracies?
- What actions would add some spice, some humor, or some excitement to the characterization?

Now it's time to pretend you are a:

*tightrope-
    walker
hair stylist
dancer
preacher
fisherman
baseball pitcher
lion tamer
disk jockey
switchboard
    operator
pianist
pizza-maker
maid*

## ANIMAL CHARACTERIZATIONS

Animal characterizations are just what they seem — the characterizing of animals. Animal characterizations require a different type of understanding and expression. You must get inside the outer coverings and really understand who or what you are before you can accurately and realistically pantomime your character. Your purpose is not simply to imitate an animal or a character, but you must communicate the "total who," including habits, feelings, instincts, actions, etc.

Consider the following: What is the personality of your animal? Are you big and bulky? Are you sleek and confident? Are you jumpy and jittery? Are your steps bold and daring or soft and cautious?

Now try on some of the following animal characterizations:

| | |
|---|---|
| *elephant* | *cow* |
| *monkey* | *rabbit* |
| *cat* | *kangaroo* |
| *puppy* | *bear* |
| *bird* | *squirrel* |
| *cougar* | *hamster* |
| *snake* | *parrot* |

# MIRROR IMAGES

Mirror images offer an excellent opportunity for
imitating and recreating movements. Ask one person
to be the leader and another person to be the reflector.
The two people face each other, and the reflector imitates the movements of the leader, as if looking into
a mirror.

Reverse roles and let the reflector become the leader.

Mimes often mirror people's actions as they engage in spontaneous performances. You should train yourself to concentrate on a person's total movement, including both bodily and facial gestures. One important rule: Be careful — be sensitive. Do not embarrass or make fun of your subject.

# ILLUSIONS

An illusion is a movement that is deceiving to the onlooker; it creates a false impression. An illusion is walking while remaining in one spot, running yet going nowhere, climbing a ladder while remaining on the ground, leaning against a wall that isn't there.

Illusions are possibly the most difficult movements to mime, and yet the most challenging and the most fun to perform once you have perfected them. Illusions are also one type of movement that you must practice to perfection before attempting to perform, because they simply do not look realistic if they are not performed well.

When learning an illusion, practice in front of a mirror. Always visualize an illusion in your mind before attempting to mime the action. A few of the more frequently used illusions are detailed on the following pages.

## A. Walking

First, *visualize,* then proceed with the following steps:

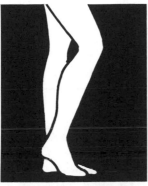

*1. Begin with your weight on the left foot, right foot beside left foot with right heel raised.*

*2. Bring right foot forward, pointing right toe.*

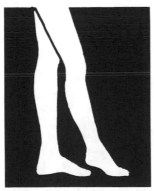

*3. Slide ball of right foot backward until even with the left foot.*

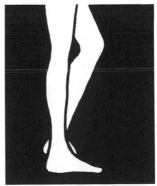

*4. Shift weight to right foot as left heel is raised.*

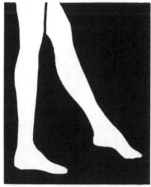

5. **Bring left foot forward, pointing left toe.**

6. **Slide ball of left foot backward until even with the right foot.**

7. **Shift weight to left foot as the right heel is raised.**

8. **Arms should take on a natural movement as when walking.**

9. **Repeat this sequence.**

There are many types of walks that can add some humor and flavor to any performance. One such comical walk is pictured below. Remember to first visualize the walk.

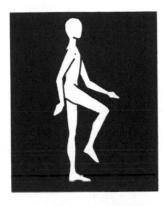

1. ***Take the beginning position — weight on left leg, left leg straight, right leg bent.***

2. ***Bend left leg slightly, flex right toe, crouch slightly.***

3. ***Extend right leg.***

4. ***Point right toe.***

**5. Place right foot for-**
**ward, pointing toe.**

**6. Slide right foot**
**back; shift weight**
**to right foot.**

## B. Climbing a Ladder

Visualize the activity.

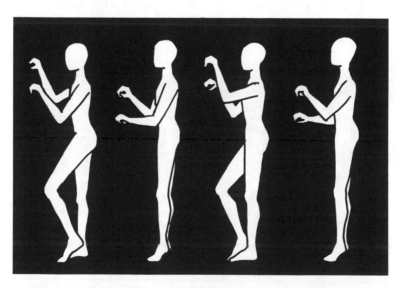

**1. Begin with weight on the right foot. Left foot is be-**
**side right foot, with the left heel raised and knee**
**bent. The right arm is up, with hand clinched in**

*a loose fist. The left arm is bent, lower than the right hand, in a loose fist.*

2. *Rise up on toes of both feet; straighten both knees. Hands are lowered to chest level, although the right is still slightly higher than the left.*

3. *Lower left foot flat on the floor, taking weight on the left foot. The right foot remains beside the left; heel is raised, knee is bent. Left hand should release its grip. Left arm is placed up, above right arm; hand is clinched in a loose fist. Right arm is bent, hand in a fist.*

4. *Rise up on toes of both feet; straighten both knees. Lower hands to chest level. Left is still slightly higher than the right. Continue the sequence.*

## C. Leaning

The illusion of leaning is different from many illusions in that it does not involve sequential movement. The illusion of leaning far to one side is accomplished by balancing your weight equally on each side of your center of gravity. Following are some pointers in creating the illusion of leaning against a wall:

- Stand with your weight on your right foot.
- Lean to the left side, with the left arm out straight, hand flat against the imaginary wall.
- To balance, cross the left leg in front of the right, pointing the toe.
- The right arm can be bent and resting on your hip.
- By shifting the head to the right, but holding it in an upright position, the illusion of leaning is further enhanced.

Leaning on a wall or other object can be projected in a slightly different way. Simply hold the left arm at shoulder level and allow the left hand to relax and hang over the imaginary object.

**1. leaning against a**
   **wall**

**2. leaning on a wall or**
   **object**

## D. Pushing

**Forward:**

Visualize this: you are attempting to push a refrigerator across the floor.

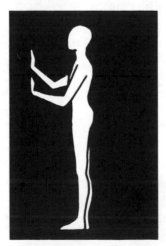

**1. Stand erect with**
   **both hands placed**
*(continued on next page)*

**2. Straighten left leg**
   **behind right. Bend**
*(continued on next page)*

| | |
|---|---|
| ***flat against the imaginary refrigerator.*** | ***right knee. "Push" body forward without moving shoulders, arms or hands. Show tension and strain in the entire body and face.*** |

## Backward:
Visualize what you will be doing.

| | |
|---|---|
| ***1. Stand erect, arms back, with both hands flat.*** | ***2. Bend knees and tuck pelvis. Shoulders should be rounded and behind the pelvis. Show tension and strain in the entire body and face.*** |

I hope that the illusions which have been detailed will give you an idea of the basic principles involved in performing illusions. After you learn the ones outlined here, you should be able to continue learning other illusions, such as climbing up a rope, running, pulling, rowing, climbing stairs, etc.

# CHAPTER 9:

# PERFORMANCE TIPS

L earning mime tricks of the trade will greatly enhance the quality of your performance. Following are some important points to emphasize as you prepare to perform:

## EXAGGERATE!
## MAGNIFY YOUR ACTIONS!

In mime, each action or gesture should be expressed with larger-than-life actions. If a mime is performing for a great number of people in a large area, his actions, and especially facial gestures, would need to be magnified even more. For example, surprise could be expressed with an open mouth and a twinkle in the eye. If being viewed by people at a greater distance, the mime should further magnify his expression by opening his mouth even wider, opening his eyes wider and raising his eyebrows, and enlarging his hand and body gestures.

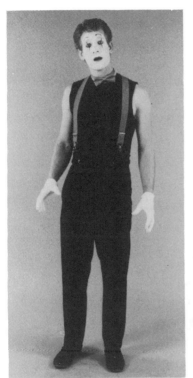

If gesturing for someone to "come here," one might simply motion with the index finger or hand. A mime should magnify his action, however, by using his entire arm, and even body movement, in addition to the finger and hand movement.

# COMMUNICATE AN IDEA, EMOTION OR THOUGHT RATHER THAN ACTING OUT WORDS

Take, for example, the phrase "I love you." If acting verbatim, a mime might point to himself (*I*), then cross his arms over his chest or point to his heart (*love*), and then point to someone (*you*). Now think about communicating the *thought* rather than acting out individual words. One might simply turn his head slightly and tuck his chin, smile, and look at the person in a special way.

Another example would be the words *come here*. If acting out the words, a mime might point to the person to whom he is beckoning (*you* is understood), gesture with his index finger (*come*), and point to a certain spot (*here*).

Now, rather than acting out the words, think about communicating the thought. A mime might simply look at the person and nod his head in the direction he wants the person to go. Another expression of the thought might be to look at the person and then adamantly point to the spot to which he wants the person to go.

Communicating through mime means that the mime must interpret beyond the words. When communicating about Jesus, the mime must understand who he is and what he is like (gentle, kind, loving, caring). With this understanding, the communication of Christ will be real.

## COMMUNICATE IN ADEQUATE DETAIL

A delicate balance must be maintained when deciding the amount of detail to be included in your actions. Too much detail would be tedious and unnecessary, and would actually take away from the thought or message you are attempting to relate. On the other hand, too little attention to detail could leave your audience wondering what is really happening.

As an example, let's imagine that I am holding an object in my hand; my hand is somewhat cupped. The object could be a baseball, a jar, an orange, a potato, a ball of yarn, etc. I now take a bite out of the object. The audience now knows that it is edible — an orange, a pear, an apple, perhaps? I now take the object, polish it on my sleeve, and take another bite. Ah-ha. An apple!

Define objects well enough and make actions detailed enough so that the audience can clearly understand what you are attempting to communicate.

# WIND UP FOR EACH ACTION

In order to focus attention on and define certain actions, it is a good practice to wind up for each action. *Windup* simply means to first move in the opposite direction of the action to be taken. For example, before

reaching forward to pick up a jar, first make an arm movement backward. Before reaching upward to pick an apple from a tree, first lower your bent arm, and then extend it upward. This windup movement emphasizes the action that is about to take place and draws the audience's attention to what is happening.

# DO NOT LET IMAGINARY OBJECTS MAGICALLY APPEAR AND DISAPPEAR

With the wave of a magic wand or the sprinkle of magic dust, a magician can make rabbits and doves appear from nowhere. A mime also has this power, but in a different sense. A mime must create objects, giving them substance and an illusion of reality.

Once the object has been created or defined, however, a mime cannot forget about it. If you open a door, you must close it. You must remember also where the door is positioned so that you do not unintentionally walk through it later. A common mistake for beginners is to take an object, use it, and then let it magically float away. This lack of concentration and forethought makes for a sloppy performance. If you pick up an object, be sure to put it somewhere.

# MAKE ACTIONS SHARP AND CLEAR, COMPLETING EACH ACTION BEFORE BEGINNING ANOTHER

When performing a sketch involving a sequence of actions, often a mime will unknowingly combine the separate tasks or movements into one long movement. This is particularly confusing for the audience since no words are spoken to help define the actions. Using a windup helps to some extent; hesitation between gestures also helps. When practicing, it is useful to actually stop between gestures. When performing, however, there can be only a slight hesitation. A mime must also make very clear, precise movements, being careful not to make wasted movements.

## FREEDOM OF EXPRESSION

There are other unwritten guidelines which many mimes follow: do not touch other actors on stage; do not use any props; never make "people" sounds. I agree that these suggestions are good for the most part. However, I feel that the main purpose is to proclaim the message of Jesus Christ, not to strictly adhere to the do's and don'ts of professional mime. I often cross these boundaries and allow for total freedom of expression.

## CHOOSING MATERIALS*

Choose your performance materials carefully and prayerfully. The pieces you use should convey some facet of the gospel or some aspect of the Christian walk. I believe also that your choices should reflect areas of the faith where you have strong beliefs and firm convictions. Don't hesitate to do materials that are very familiar to you and to others. Material drawn directly from scripture is probably one of the best sources. I use songs (taped or live) and original stories that teach principles

*Following four sections excerpted from the filmstrip reference script of *The Art of Pantomime in the Church,* © copyright 1982 Meriwether Publishing Ltd. (Colorado Springs, CO), pp. 2-4.

of living in the kingdom of God. Songs chosen should have clear diction (solo vocals without a lot of backup group tend to allow the message to come across well), and the images in the songs should not be so abstract that they can't somehow be interpreted in movement. Stories should have a good deal of action so there are not long times when the performer must wait for the next move. The use of music and sound effects in the recording of story or scripture tapes will greatly enhance the final production and make the job of the performer easier by helping to create moods and objects.

# PREPARATION OF PERFORMER AND PROGRAM

Use your whole body at all times. Pantomime is much more than hand and face expression. I like to think of my body as a three-dimensional sphere of action in space rather than as an upright stick moving about on the ground. I like to utilize the full capacity of that sphere. If I reach my right hand out, the whole top half of my body shifts forward as my left leg shifts back and my right knee bends to extend my reach. If, as is often the case, an isolated movement of the head, arm, eye, etc., would be the most effective, the rest of the body is intensely involved by not moving at all! The pantomime artist reacts with his whole body, indeed, with his whole being. In working solo, I play all the characters, changing by turning fully around and returning to face the audience with a different facial expression and body attitude. In a company situation, there may be a performer for each character. Some may play several characters; some may play non-person roles (animal, wall, tree, etc.). Background vocals may also be done by live readers or singers.

Cultivate and use your ability to visualize the places and objects portrayed in the pantomime. Your own sense of the reality of these imaginary surroundings will carry over to the audience. You must then reinforce their (and your own) conception by the way you touch and hold objects (showing their texture, shape and weight) and consistently observe the conventions you have established. Don't walk through walls or move doors from one place to another! The pantomime medium does, however, allow for a complete change of setting in a flash when the piece calls for it. You open a door and suddenly, without moving through space more than a foot, you are in a woodland setting. The same two arms that at one moment are cradling the sweet baby Jesus are in the next moment rising to form the stiff shape of the cross, and in yet the next are joined at the wrist to become the wings of the dove on its descent to the heart of the waiting believer! Time and space can disappear with the imaginative use of pantomime.

Since there is no absolutely right or wrong way to express things in pantomime, you may experiment during rehearsals with different ways of showing certain objects or attitudes. But when performance time comes, you should have repeated your final version enough so that you and your fellow performers can execute moves with confidence and assurance. Movements in pantomime must be precise and assertive. The audience becomes very quickly attuned to the fact that the primary medium here is movement. If you "slur" your movement, it will have the same effect as when a speaking actor slurs his speech.

## SETTING AND SET PROPS

Really look at the church for the most appropriate setting. If there is no good place, or the good place is not available to you, make the most of the space you are given by creating a stage area. Place the audience chairs in a semicircle around the performance area; aim a couple of clamp floodlights or spotlights (attached to empty mike stands, music stands, chair backs or whatever is available) from right and left front toward the performance area. If you have no stage set or backdrop, use as uncluttered a wall as possible; inappropriate objects in your background will force your audience to visually "edit" out what isn't supposed to be there. Try to get your performance area (or part of it) above floor level.

I have used choir risers, portable stages, even a sturdy tabletop! Test everything in advance so that it works the way you want it to. Many churches have an actual stage that may be in use for storage of athletic equipment or outdated Sunday school materials. Reclaim it (tactfully)!

# FINAL TIPS

Give yourself plenty of preparation time before performance. I allow two hours for make-up, costume and last-minute physical warm-ups. Since pantomime is such a highly visual medium, the visual effect you create — your image — is a vital part of the program. Give yourself time to do a precise job of your make-up. Make sure you also have plenty of light and a good mirror large enough so you can occasionally stand back a step and still see your whole face. Clown white greasepaint makes a very opaque and professional-looking whiteface. Once you have applied it (not too thick but evenly covered), you need to powder it (any white cosmetic or baby powder will do) before putting other finishing touches on. Pancake whiteface make-up is a little faster to apply and comes off somewhat easier, but it doesn't cover your natural skin color as well, nor does it stand up as well to theatrical lighting. I've found that commercial non-smear liquid eyeliner works best for the black around eyes and other markings. It is not a good idea, however, to use the brush that comes in the bottle. Buy yourself some good-quality make-up brushes! Your costume should be kept fairly simple, especially if you will be playing several characters. Let your body language say who you are, possibly supplemented with a simple costume piece. The neutrality of a black leotard makes it a popular costume, but many of us do not feel at all comfortable in only a leotard! White coveralls have also become widely used and do allow for great freedom of movement while maintaining a fairly trim look. I have found that a very workable costume can be made by combining white elastic-top pants (available at any nursing outfitters) with a waist-length long-sleeved tunic of a solid color. White gloves are a little hard to find, but most formal-wear shops sell them, and band directors usually have a source they'll share with you. Shoes should be plain, light and very flexible; check out the dance supply store and the nursing outfitter. Some athletic shoes will do, but it is difficult to find a pair that doesn't attract a lot of attention.

The most important tip I have for you is to pray before you perform. The whole process of developing the character and the program should be bathed in prayer, but especially before you step out to minister with the gift God has given you, yield yourself consciously to him and trust that he will use you in his service. And have fun: "Rejoice in the Lord always, again I say rejoice!"

# CHAPTER 10:

# SONG
# INTERPRETATIONS

Some of the most moving and uplifting moments that I have experienced have come through mime interpretations of various songs. The process of creating a mime interpretation of a song is much the same as interpreting a scripture verse:

- Select a song.
- Read the words aloud a dozen or so times.
- Listen to the recorded music to feel the tempo and flow of words.
- Experiment with different facial expressions and body movements for each thought.
- Consider lighting and special effects.
- Put it all together and ask several people to critique your final presentation.

The songs which I have interpreted in mime have been songs which moved me in a very special way or filled a need at a particular time in my life.

While attending the Southern Baptist Convention in Los Angeles several years ago, I experienced, as did thousands of others, the magnificent power of the Holy Spirit as Sandi Patti sang "We Shall Behold Him."

With grace and beauty, she began signing (sign language) the chorus as she sang, adding a new dimension and meaning to the already-powerful words.

Below is a mime interpretation which I wrote following that experience, using a combination of sign language and other interpretative movements. The appropriate movements are in parentheses under the words they illustrate.

## *"We Shall Behold Him"**

**The sky**
*(Begin with arms outstretched toward the sky and looking upward.)*

**shall unfold,**
*(Hands make a rolling movement from the sky down in front of the body.)*

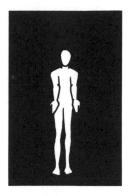

**Preparing His entrance.**
*(Hands are out-stretched in front.)*

**The stars shall applaud Him**
*(With arms up, open and close fingers as if flipping something.)*

**With thunders of Praise.**
*(Hit palms together in front of chest and then raise hands upward.)*

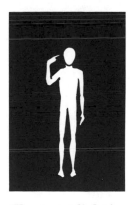

**The sweet light in His eyes**
*(Draw both hands down, stopping right hand at eye level, fingers relaxed and pointing to right eye.)*

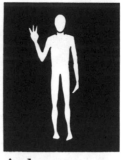

**Shall enhance
those awaiting,**
*(Stretch right hand
out in front of body,
then draw outward
to right side. Then
draw left hand out
and to the left side.)*

**And we**
*(Form a **W** with
the three middle
fingers of the right
hand. With right
hand at right shoul-
der, make a half-
circle with hand in
front of body, end-
ing with hand at
left shoulder.)*

**shall**
*(With right hand
at right side of face
and fingers spread
apart, move the
hand forward us-
ing only the wrist.)*

**behold**
*(Using right hand,
make a **V** with in-
dex and middle
finger. Point the **V**
toward the eyes and
then rotate the
hand outward and
upward, stretching
right arm toward
sky.)*

**Him,**
*(Draw open hand downward, with the thumb passing in front of forehead, nose and chin, and stopping at chest level.)*

**Then, face**
*(Hold right hand open over face.)*

**to**
*(Touch right and left index fingers together.)*

**face.**
*(Place right hand over face again and then rotate hand outward and up, palm facing sky.)*

**We**
*(Form a **W** with the three middle fingers of the right hand. With right hand at right shoulder, make a half-circle with hand in front of body, ending with hand at left shoulder.)*

**shall**
*(With right hand at right side of face and fingers spread apart, move the hand forward using only the wrist.)*

**behold**
*(Using right hand, make a V with index and middle finger. Point the V toward the eyes and then rotate the hand outward and upward, stretching right arm toward sky.)*

**Him,**
*(Draw open hand downward, with the thumb passing in front of forehead, nose and chin, and stopping at chest level.)*

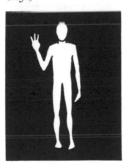

**we**
*(Form a W with the three middle fingers of the right hand. With right hand at right shoulder, make a half-circle with hand in front of body, ending with hand at left shoulder.)*

**shall**
*(With right hand at right side of face and fingers spread apart, move the hand forward using only the wrist.)*

**behold**
*(Using right hand, make a V with index and middle finger. Point the V toward the eyes and then rotate the hand outward and upward, stretching right arm toward sky.)*

**Him**
*(Draw open hand downward, with the thumb passing in front of forehead, nose and chin, and stopping at chest level.)*

**Face**
*(Hold right hand
open over face.)*

**to**
*(Touch right and
left index fingers
together.)*

**face**
*(Place right hand
over face again and
then rotate hand
outward and up,
palm facing sky.)*

**in all of His glory.**
*(Starting with arms
at sides, raise arms
slowly upward,
moving fingers
rapidly.)*

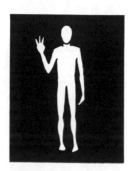 

**We**
*(Form a **W** with the three middle fingers of the right hand. With right hand at right shoulder, make a half-circle with hand in front of body, ending with hand at left shoulder.)*

**shall**
*(With right hand at right side of face and fingers spread apart, move the hand forward using only the wrist.)*

**behold**
*(Using right hand,
make a **V** with in-
dex and middle
finger. Point the **V**
toward the eyes and
then rotate the hand
outward and up-
ward, stretching
right arm toward
sky.)*

**Him,**
*(Draw open hand
downward, with the
thumb passing in
front of forehead,
nose and chin, and
stopping at chest
level.)*

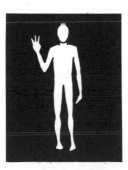

**we**
*(Form a **W** with the
three middle fingers
of the right hand.
With right hand at
right shoulder, make
a half-circle with
hand in front of
body, ending with
hand at left shoul-
der.)*

**shall**
*(With right hand
at right side of face
and fingers spread
apart, move the
hand forward using
only the wrist.)*

**behold**
*(Using right hand, make a V with index and middle finger. Point the V toward the eyes and then rotate the hand outward and upward, stretching right arm toward sky.)*

**Him**
*(Draw open hand downward, with the thumb passing in front of forehead, nose and chin, and stopping at chest level.)*

**Face**
*(Hold right hand open over face.)*

**to**
*(Touch right and left index fingers together.)*

**face,**
*(Place right hand
over face again and
then rotate hand
outward and up,
palm facing sky.)*

**our savior**
*(Cross arms in front
of body at chest
level, then draw
arms down to sides.)*

**and Lord.**
*(With right hand,
make an L with
thumb and index
finger. Place L hand
at left shoulder and
then bring hand
down to right side.)*

**The angels shall
sound the shout of
His coming.**

*(Place open hands
at mouth and then
bring hands out and
up, as if tracing the
shape of a large
megaphone. Repeat
a couple of times.)*

**The sleeping shall rise from their slumbering place;**
*(Begin with arms at sides, palms facing forward. Slowly raise arms toward sky.)*

**And those who remain**
*(Stretch right hand out in front of body, then draw hand outward to right side. Repeat with left hand to left side.)*

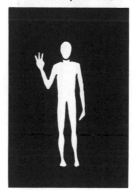

**shall be changed in a moment;**
*(Move arms and hands several times randomly in and out in front of body.)*

**And we**
*(Form a **W** with the three middle fingers of the right hand. With right hand at right shoulder, make a half-circle with hand in front of body, ending with hand at left shoulder.)*

**shall**
*(With right hand at right side of face and fingers spread apart, move the hand forward using only the wrist.)*

**behold**
*(Using right hand, make a **V** with index and middle finger. Point the **V** toward the eyes and then rotate hand outward and upward, stretching right arm toward sky.)*

**Him,**
*(Draw open hand downward, with the thumb passing in front of forehead, nose and chin, and stopping at chest level.)*

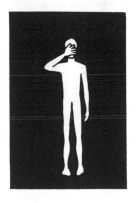

**then, face**
*(Hold right hand open over face.)*

**to**
*(Touch right and index fingers together.)*

**face.**
*(Place right hand over face again and then rotate hand outward and up, palm facing sky.)*

**We**
*(Form a **W** with the three middle fingers of the right hand. With right hand at right shoulder, make a half-circle with hand in front of body, ending with hand at left shoulder.)*

**shall**
*(With right hand at right side of face and fingers spread apart, move the hand forward using only the wrist.)*

**behold**
*(Using right hand, make a **V** with in- dex and middle finger. Point the **V** toward the eyes and then rotate the hand outward and upward, stretching right arm toward sky.)*

**Him,**
*(Draw open hand downward, with the thumb passing in front of forehead, nose and chin, and stopping at chest level.)*

**we**
*(Form a **W** with the three middle fingers of the right hand. With right hand at right shoulder, make a half-circle with hand in front of body, ending with hand at left shoulder.)*

**shall**
*(With right hand at right side of face and fingers spread apart, move the hand forward using only the wrist.)*

**behold**
*(Using right hand, make a **V** with index and middle finger. Point the **V** toward the eyes and then rotate the hand outward and upward, stretching right arm toward sky.)*

**Him**
*(Draw open hand downward, with the thumb passing in front of forehead, nose and chin, and stopping at chest level.)*

**Face**
*(Hold right hand open over face.)*

**to**
*(Touch right and left index fingers together.)*

**face**
*(Place right hand over face again and then rotate hand outward and up, palm facing sky.)*

**in all of His glory.**
*(Starting with arms at sides, raise arms slowly upward, moving fingers rapidly.)*

**We**
*(Form a **W** with the three middle fingers of the right hand. With right hand at right shoulder, make a half-circle with hand in front of body, ending with hand at left shoulder.)*

**shall**
*(With right hand at right side of face and fingers spread apart, move the hand forward using only the wrist.)*

**behold**
*(Using right hand, make a V with in- dex and middle finger. Point the V toward the eyes and then rotate the hand outward and up- ward, stretching right arm toward sky.)*

**Him,**
*(Draw open hand downward, with the thumb passing in front of forehead, nose and chin, and stop- ping at chest level.)*

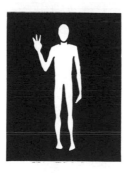

**we**
*(Form a W with the three middle fingers of the right hand. With right hand at right shoulder, make a half-circle with hand in front of body, ending with hand at left shoulder.)*

**shall**
*(With right hand at right side of face and fingers spread apart, move the hand for- ward using only the wrist.)*

**behold**

*(Using right hand, make a **V** with index and middle finger. Point the **V** toward the eyes and then rotate the hand outward and upward, stretching right arm toward sky.)*

**Him**

*(Draw open hand downward, with the thumb passing in front of forehead, nose and chin, and stopping at chest level.)*

**Face**

*(Hold right hand open over face.)*

**to**

*(Touch right and left index fingers together.)*

**face,**
*(Place right hand
over face again and
then rotate hand
outward and up,
palm facing sky.)*

**our savior and Lord.**
*(From* savior *posi-
tion of arms crossed
in front of body,
slowly stretch arms*

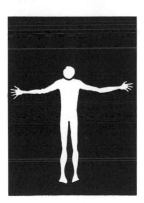

*outward to sides
at shoulder level.
Slowly open hands
and finally drop
head forward.)*

Another song which has a powerful message that can be enhanced by the use of mime is "God Gave the Song." The words tell about God's giving the world a song (which is Jesus).

A spotlight is needed for this mime, as is a cross (placed somewhere on the stage). The spotlight as used in this mime is symbolic of the "song." The detailed movements for this interpretive mime follow:

## *"God Gave the Song"\**

As the music begins, the room or sanctuary should be fairly dark. Some light is needed so that the characters can be seen, but dark enough so the spotlight can be seen. The spot should be small.

After the music has been playing about 30 seconds, flash the spotlight on a side wall, as far back as possible. The spotlight should be moved in a bouncing motion with the tempo of the music. Gradually work the spot toward the front of the sanctuary.

About one minute after the song begins, several mimes enter from the back. They watch the spot with a great deal of curiosity and uncertainty, and begin moving with it. Just prior to narration in the song, the spot must become stationary at the front of the sanctuary against a solid background, such as the front of the pulpit or on a wall. When the narration begins, the mimes act out the narration in relation to the spotlight (which is the "song").

*"God Gave the Song," words by William J. and Gloria Gaither, and Ron Huff, music by William J. Gaither and Ron Huff. © Copyright 1969, 1973 by Gaither Music Company/ASCAP and Paragon Music Corporation/ASCAP. International copyright secured. All rights reserved. Used by permission.

**The song came
into our world
through a manger.**

**Some tried to
ignore it.**

**Others tried to
change the tune.**

*(As if turning a
wheel. Spot can
change colors with
each turn.)*

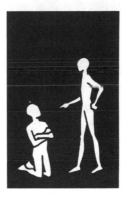

**They made laws
to stop it.**

**Armies marched against it.**

**They killed some who sang the song.**

**They screamed at it in fury.**

**They tried to drown it out.**

**They nailed it to a tree.**
*(Actors throw the spotlight onto a cross. The light changes to red.)*

**That should do it.**

When the narration says, "but it didn't," the music begins again. The spotlight begins slowly bouncing. As the music gets broader, the spot should make broad sweeps across the front of the auditorium. The spot should then "land" on the actors, one by one, to symbolize Jesus entering their hearts.

**But it didn't.**

*(spot landing on hearts)*

As the music fades, the actors exit.

# CHAPTER 11:

# SCRIPTURE
# INTERPRETATIONS

**D**ramatization of scriptures can be a beautiful part of a worship experience. A mime who can visually express his feelings and understanding of the scriptures can be a powerful instrument of interpretation, bringing the audience a new and deeper meaning of the words. Included in this section is an idea for a mime interpretation of Genesis 1:1-5. The fun and satisfaction of mime really comes, however, as you, yourself, create and then express that which you have created, for in creating, a mime is involved in an exciting and rewarding process.

How do I create my own scripture interpretation using mime?

- Select a scripture — a psalm, a parable, a lesson.
- Read the scripture aloud a dozen or more times. Read with expression. Emphasize different parts until one feels right.
- Make a cassette recording of your final version of this scripture.
- Experiment with a variety of facial expressions and body movements for each thought. (Remember: Do not mime each

word, such as: "In – the – beginning – God – created – the . . ." Also, do not decide on a particular movement until you put all the movements together. One movement might or might not flow smoothly to the next movement. Some combinations will work together better than others.)

- Consider and experiment with possible background music, background movements, lighting and special effects to complement the interpretation.
- Put it all together!
- Have a few people critique your presentation. Graciously accept their criticism — positive and negative. But remember, just because someone tells you to do something differently, that doesn't mean you have to change it. It's your interpretation!

Following is a mime interpretation of Genesis 1:1-5:

## *Genesis 1:1-5*
*(King James Version)*

*In the beginning, God created the heaven*       *and the earth.*

*And the earth was without form, and void;*

*and darkness was upon the face of the deep.*

*And the Spirit of God moved upon the face of the waters.*

*And God said, Let there be light;*

*and there was light.*
*And God saw the*
*light, that it was*
*good:*

*and God divided the*
*light from the dark-*
*ness.*

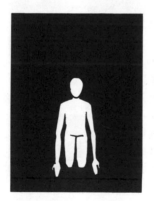

*And God called the*
*light Day, and the*
*darkness he called*
*Night.*

*And the evening and*
*the morning were*
*the first day.*

Following are several interpretive mime skits dramatizing teachings from the scripture without being tied line for line to specific verses.

## Scripture Skit #1

# The Gardener*

**NUMBER OF MIMES:**   four

**CHARACTERS:**   two gardeners

two trees

*(Two gardeners, each pulling his baby tree, go to Centerstage.)*

**GARDENER #1:**   **Digs a hole, plops his tree in the hole, covers the roots with dirt, and then exits.**

**GARDENER #2:**   **Digs a hole, carefully plants his tree, gently covers the roots with dirt, waters the tree, and then exits.**

**GARDENER #1:**   **Enters, looks at the tree, dumps a bucket of water over his tree, then exits.** *(TREE #1 can give a humorous response to being drowned.)*

**GARDENER #2:**   **Enters, hoes the weeds from around the tree, waters it, then exits.** *(TREE #2 is growing.)*

**GARDENER #1:**   **Enters, scolds his tree for not growing like the other tree. Finally, in disgust, he kicks dirt at his plant, then exits.** *(TREE #1 is dying from lack of care.)*

**GARDENER #2:**   **Enters, obviously pleased with his flowering tree, pampers it, weeds around it, waters it, fertilizes it. He starts to exit when he notices the other tree is dying. He looks around to make sure that GARDENER #1 isn't coming, and then he begins weeding around it and waters it. TREE #1 offers a**

---

*Performance rights for this skit are granted with the purchase of this book. No further permission is needed to adapt or integrate this skit within any performance situation for mime ministry.

**hint that it might survive. GARDENER #2 exits.**

*SCRIPTURE THOUGHT:* Before a plant can grow, it must receive certain essentials to help it in the growth process: fertile soil, water, sunlight and some TLC. This tender loving care includes keeping weeds from choking the plant, keeping bugs from damaging the leaves and fruit, and adding any fertilizer that is necessary for growth. These components determine whether the plant will live.

People are just like the plant in that their fruitfulness depends much on the nurturing which they receive. Children need to be bathed in love, kindness, understanding, affection, hope and laughter. As children receive these, they will, in turn, learn to give them. Another kind of nurturing which children need is pointed out in Ephesians 6:4, where parents are told to "bring them up in the nurture and admonition of the Lord." New Christians also need to be nurtured as they begin their Christian journey, for they will face many droughts and many weeds trying to choke them out.

## *Scripture Skit #2*

# Grand Opening*

*NUMBER OF MIMES:* minimum of five

*CHARACTERS:* one store manager
four or more for the group

*(The skit begins with one mime [the STORE MANAGER] standing beside an easel, holding a sign that reads:*

*Performance rights for this skit are granted with the purchase of this book. No further permission is needed to adapt or integrate this skit within any performance situation for mime ministry.

```
GRAND OPENING
FREE SURPRISES
TO THE FIRST
100 PEOPLE
```

*The mime is inviting all to come in and visit the store.)*
A group of mimes enters, trying to find out what all the
commotion is about. After reading the sign, they all
get excited. They walk to the back of the imaginary
line of people. The first mime in the line happens to
be the smallest in the group — also the shyest and
the quietest. The smallest mime shows no concern
over getting into the store first, but the others in
the group obviously are concerned. One by one, the
mimes in the group gradually work their way in front
of the smallest mime, and try to get in front of each
other. Finally, they reach the door of the store, and
the first mime is allowed to go inside. As he exits
from another door, licking an ice cream cone, the
next mime is invited into the store. One by one, the
mimes enter the store and exit with an ice cream
cone (imaginary, of course).

When it comes time for the smallest mime to
enter, the STORE MANAGER motions for him to
wait. He then indicates that the 100th person has just
gone inside. As the smallest mime stands watching,
he is somewhat disappointed, but makes no big fuss.
The group of mimes is laughing and eating and having a great time; the mimes do not even notice that
their friend has been left out. The smallest mime turns

to leave, but the STORE MANAGER grabs his arm and tells him to wait. The STORE MANAGER turns the sign around and it reads:

THE 101ˢᵀ PERSON WILL RECEIVE ONE FREE ICE CREAM CONE EACH DAY FOR A YEAR!

The smallest mime can't believe it! "Surely not me," he mimes. "Yes," the STORE MANAGER indicates, and hands him a large ice cream cone. The other mimes, seeing what has happened, show disappointment. Even their ice cream doesn't taste as good as it did before. All exit.

SCRIPTURE THOUGHT: In Mark 9:35, we read Christ's words as he spoke to his disciples: "If any man desires to be first, the same shall be last of all, and servant of all." In Matthew 19:30, Christ's words to his disciple are, "but many that are first, shall be last; and the last shall be first."

## *Scripture Skit #3*

### The Puzzle*

NUMBER OF MIMES:    five
CHARACTERS:    one mime called SOLO
group of four mimes
PROPS:    a large cardboard heart cut into five pieces, with the
words *YOU ARE SPECIAL* written on the heart
recording of "Puzzles" from the musical *Down by the*

---

*Performance rights for this skit are granted with the purchase of this book. No further permission is needed to adapt or integrate this skit within any performance situation for mime ministry.

*Creekbank,* Impact Records

The skit begins with one mime *(SOLO)* sitting off to the side of
the stage, curiously examining a large tear-shaped
piece of cardboard. A group of four mimes enters,
playing with a beachball *(imaginary or real)*. **SOLO**
watches excitedly as the group plays and laughs.
The ball is accidentally thrown over the head of one
in the group. **SOLO** jumps up and runs after the ball,
only to trip and fall on the ball, completely deflating it.
**SOLO** expresses sorrow and regret over the accident,
but the group does not accept his apology.

They return to Centerstage where they find
four pieces of cardboard on the floor. They begin
looking at the pieces; at first they don't know what
to do with the pieces, but they finally begin trying
to fit the pieces together. They get frustrated when
the pieces don't fit. Finally, one mime in the group
realizes that SOLO is holding a piece of the puzzle.
He runs over to SOLO and beckons him to bring his
piece of the puzzle over to the group. Although still
somewhat uncertain of the group, SOLO eases over
to the group and fits his piece of the puzzle into the
heart. The group and SOLO read the words on the heart.
The group now realizes that each one is important in

making the puzzle complete. They hug SOLO and all exit, expressing happiness in their completeness.

**OPTIONAL ENDING:**  Play the song "Puzzles."

**SCRIPTURE THOUGHT:**  I Corinthians 12 is the basis for this skit. Each of us is that missing piece of puzzle! We are, each of us, one of God's special creations. We are each unique. We each have special gifts and abilities. God wants each of us to use our talents and abilities to edify the church and glorify him. We are also to recognize the beauty and worth of every individual. Too many times we shun those who are not like us; we even go so far as to put them down. God wants our attitude to be one of love and acceptance of all.

## Scripture Skit #4

# The Tennis Match*

**NUMBER OF MIMES:**  four

**CHARACTERS:**  All are spectators at a tennis match.

**PROPS:**  four chairs or a long bench, set Centerstage, facing the audience

(*Optional*) a soundtrack of a tennis ball being hit

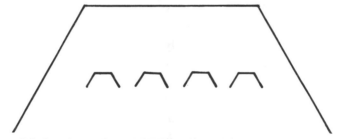

**The skit begins when MIME #1 enters and sits down in chair #1** (*Stage Left*) **to watch a tennis match. He turns**

---

*Performance rights for this skit are granted with the purchase of this book. No further permission is needed to adapt or integrate this skit within any performance situation for mime ministry.

his head from side to side, as if watching the players hit the ball back and forth. MIME #1 shows little emotion or expression — his actions are stiff and mechanical.

After MIME #1 has watched a couple of serves, MIME #2 enters and sits down in chair #2. MIME #2 joins in with the same back-and-forth head movements, but MIME #2 is more emotional, cheering, etc. MIME #1 gives MIME #2 some disapproving looks, however. Gradually, MIME #2 becomes more staid and eventually conforms to the stiff, emotionless actions of MIME #1. *(MIME #1 and MIME #2 must make the exact same moves.)*

MIME #3 enters and sits in chair #3. MIME #3 is really into the game, jumping up, cheering, etc. However, after some disapproving looks from MIMES #1 & 2, MIME #3 also conforms to the mechanical, emotionless actions.

MIME #4 enters and sits in chair #4 *(Stage Right)*. He obviously loves tennis and is very excited to be at the match. He cheers, claps, laughs — just has a grand ol' time. MIMES #1, 2 & 3 give him disapproving looks, but MIME #4 doesn't lose his enthusiasm; in fact, he tries to get them more excited. Gradually, we see MIMES #2 & 3 regain their enthusiasm, but MIME #1 maintains his staid personality.

The match is finally over; MIMES #2, 3 & 4 exit. MIME #1 rises and haughtily exits. *(Many humorous actions can be added to this skit. For example, MIME #1 can do some things which MIMES #2 & 3 mimic, such as crossing a leg, hiccupping, sneezing, etc. Remember that MIMES #2 & 3 become clones of MIME #1.)*

**SCRIPTURE THOUGHT:** In Romans 12:2, we read, "and be not conformed to this world . . . " In our society, we find external pressures are great. Everywhere we turn, we are bombarded with temptations to join in with those things which we believe to be wrong. Peer pressure to conform and "go along with the crowd" is a constant force. Too often, to get off the hook, we compromise a little, and then a little more, until we have finally compromised ourselves into a new set of values.

The verse in Romans 12 goes on to say, "but be ye transformed by the renewing of your mind." This renewing of the mind comes as we place our trust in God, as we study God's Word, and as we pray for God's guidance and strength to be firm in our convictions.

Peer pressure is great, but God is greater!

# CHAPTER 12:

# MIME SKITS WITH A MESSAGE

**M**ime skits with a Christian message are difficult to find. Due to the lack of material, I have always written my own skits (see Resources). A variety of resources can be used in writing skits, such as children's stories, Scripture verses and real-life situations.

After I or my group performs a skit, I usually follow up with a verbal application of the story to daily living. In this way, I am sure the audience understands the message I have attempted to communicate. Included in this chapter are several skits which I hope you will enjoy performing, followed by a scriptural thought to help you in making a verbal application.

## *Message Skit #1*

# The Rebel*

***NUMBER OF MIMES:*** two or four

***PROPS:*** ladder, table or chair

---

*Performance rights for this skit are granted with the purchase of this book. No further permission is needed to adapt or integrate this skit within any performance situation for mime ministry.

**SETTING:** Mime #1 is a PUPPETEER; should be standing on a ladder, table or chair. Mime #2 is a MARIONETTE; should be standing in front and below the PUPPETEER.

**PUPPETEER enters, dragging MARIONETTE by his back collar, and places the MARIONETTE in front of the ladder. PUPPETEER climbs the ladder and takes hold of the wooden handles** *(Imaginary)* **controlling the MARIONETTE'S strings** *(Also imaginary).* **PUPPETEER begins trying to make MARIONETTE move around. MARIONETTE is determined not to do what the PUPPETEER wants and rebels against each attempt at control. The harder the PUPPETEER tries, the more the MARIONETTE rebels. The MARIONETTE finally gets all tangled up.**

    **PUPPETEER climbs down from the ladder and gently untangles the strings. PUPPETEER climbs back up and begins moving the MARIONETTE. This time, MARIONETTE decides to let PUPPETEER be in control. Things go smoothly. Then the PUPPETEER climbs down and gives MARIONETTE the control handle. PUPPETEER climbs back up on the ladder and watches. MARIONETTE moves on his own. Both exit.**

**OPTIONAL:** Use two puppeteers and two marionettes. Have the marionettes trying to do something together; they will become entangled as one rebels against his controller.

**SCRIPTURE THOUGHT:** Acts 10 contains a passage in which Peter was called by God to minister to Cornelius, a Gentile. Peter refused at first, but finally surrendered to the Lord's instructions. Afterwards, not only did Cornelius follow God, but his entire family did, also. If we only surrender to God's will and surrender to his control, we will receive a new freedom never before experienced.

## Message Skit #2

# Pleasing Others*

**NUMBER OF MIMES:**  six

**MIME #1** *(PAINTER)* **and MIME #6 enter, carrying paint can and paintbrush** *(Imaginary)*. **MIME #6 indicates that PAINTER should paint a huge wall** *(Extended across the stage)*. **MIME #6 leaves. PAINTER gets his equipment ready** *(Opens can, stirs paint, etc.)* **and begins painting a large imaginary wall with up-and-down strokes.**

**MIME #2 enters. PAINTER and MIME #2 speak to each other, and then PAINTER resumes his painting. MIME #2 steps back and watches for a moment. He then steps up to PAINTER and suggests that he paint with side-to-side strokes rather than up-and-down strokes. PAINTER thanks him for his suggestion and begins painting the same place again, this time with side-to-side strokes. MIME #2 exits.**

**MIME #3 enters. After MIME #3 and PAINTER nod to each other, MIME #3 watches PAINTER for a moment, and then suggests that he paint with up-and-down strokes. PAINTER, following his suggestion, begins again, painting over where he has already painted. MIME #3 exits.**

**MIME #4 enters. MIME #4 and PAINTER exchange greetings. As PAINTER continues working, MIME #4 indicates that he has an idea. He leaves and returns with a roller and pan** *(Imaginary)*. **PAINTER feels this is a good idea and follows his suggestion, rolling paint side to side. MIME #4 exits.**

**MIME #5 enters. He watches PAINTER for a few**

*Performance rights for this skit are granted with the purchase of this book. No further permission is needed to adapt or integrate this skit within any performance situation for mime ministry.

– 147 –

moments and then begins laughing. PAINTER is curious as to why he is laughing. MIME #5 shows him that he should be rolling up and down instead of side to side. PAINTER agrees and begins again, this time rolling up and down.

MIME #6 re-enters to see what kind of job PAINTER has done. MIME #6 can't believe PAINTER has covered so little of the wall. He points to his watch and motions that PAINTER should have already had the entire wall painted.

PAINTER indicates he is sorry — he tried — and could he please be paid for what he did paint. MIME #6 simply laughs and motions *no way*. MIME #6 exits. PAINTER exits.

*SCRIPTURE THOUGHT:* Many times we are so busy trying to please others that we fail to examine our own value system in order to make decisions we feel are right. Samson tried to please Delilah and ended up paying a high price for his weakness.

## *Message Skit #3*
## Golf Game*

*NUMBER OF MIMES:* two

*SETTING:* Mime #1 *(TEACHER)* is going to teach Mime #2 *(STUDENT)* how to hit a golf ball.

Both mimes enter, each carrying an imaginary bag of golf clubs. TEACHER lays down his bag, stretches out his arms and gets ready to hit the golf ball. STUDENT watches TEACHER closely and imitates all of his

---

*Performance rights for this skit are granted with the purchase of this book. No further permission is needed to adapt or integrate this skit within any performance situation for mime ministry.

**actions** *(Although not too gracefully).*

TEACHER next prepares to demonstrate hitting a golf ball. He selects a club, places the ball on the tee, gets his feet set, etc., and then hits the ball. Both mimes watch the ball go a great distance. TEACHER is obviously proud of his hit, and STUDENT certainly is impressed.

STUDENT now prepares to hit his own ball. He selects a club, places the ball on the tee, gets his feet set, and then swings at the ball. Both mimes stare at the ball, still sitting on the tee. TEACHER moves STUDENT a little and motions for him to try again. And so begins a series of attempts on the part of the STUDENT to hit the ball. A variety of funny things can happen with each swing: STUDENT backswings too far and falls down; STUDENT lets go of the club and it flies out into the audience; STUDENT hits the ball, but it rolls only a few feet. Ad-lib with your own ideas.

The TEACHER, meanwhile, starts out patient and understanding, but gradually turns into an impatient, raving tyrant.

The ends comes when the TEACHER begins breaking his golf clubs and just loses control of himself. He exits. STUDENT is puzzled by his TEACHER'S actions, but he finally breaks his own golf club and exits.

*SCRIPTURE THOUGHT:* Proverbs 25:28 (King James Version) reads, "He that hath no rule over his own spirit is like a city that is broken down, and without walls." Self-control should be a characteristic of the spirit-filled Christian. We will certainly fail sometimes, but we should try to imitate Christ's life as much as possible.

## Message Skit #4

# Power Source*

**NUMBER OF MIMES:** five

**PROPS:** a lantern, a flashlight, some matches, a candle, a lamp base with a light bulb

**SETTING:** Stage should be dimly lit.

**MIME #1 enters, holding a lighted lantern. He stands back and off to one side of the stage.** *(This mime is symbolic of Jesus.)*

**MIME #2 enters, holding an unlighted candle, and is groping through the darkness. MIME #1 steps forward, holds out his lantern, and beckons MIME #2 to come to him. MIME #2 looks at the lantern, then his candle, and indicates that he is considering going to MIME #1.**

**Suddenly, MIME #3 enters and is very flashy with his flashlight. His light looks so much more appealing than Jesus' light. MIME #2 decides to go to the flashlight. He attempts to light his candle from the flashlight. When his candle will not light, he accidently turns off the flashlight. When the light goes off, he is confused. MIME #3 takes the flashlight and turns the light on again. MIME #2 is startled when the light comes back on. He finally decides he can't trust this light and he moves away from MIME #3, who then exits.**

**Once again, MIME #1 steps forward and holds out his lantern toward MIME #2. MIME #2 then sees MIME #4 enter, carrying a lamp base and a light bulb. MIME #4 plugs in the cord to an electric outlet**

or an extension cord. Presto! A bright light comes on. MIME #2 is in awe of the bright light. MIME #2 excitedly runs over to the electric light and, curious, checks it out. He then gets the bright idea to "plug in" his candle. *(Caution:* do not *actually touch the wick to the current — only make it look that way.)* When MIME #2 plugs in his candle, he obviously receives an electric shock. *(Ad-lib comical effect here.)* MIME #2 finally gets loose from the current and quickly gets away from MIME #4. MIME #4 exits.

MIME #5 enters with a pack of matches in hand. MIME #2 watches MIME #5 strike the matches. He then walks over to MIME #5 and, several times, attempts to light his candle from the match. He gets frustrated because the match light keeps going out. *(MIME #5 can turn in such a way that he can blow out the match without the audience's seeing.)* MIME #5 exits. MIME #2 gives up.

MIME #1 once again steps forward, holding out the lantern. MIME #2 turns and sees the lantern. At first he only *sees* the lantern, but then he becomes drawn to it. MIME #2 falls on his knees and bows his head. He then rises and holds up his candle. MIME #1 takes the globe off the lantern and allows MIME #2 to light his candle. Both turn and exit, MIME #2 following MIME #1.

*SCRIPTURE THOUGHT:* We go through life constantly searching for a source of power to guide our lives. Most often, we try to draw from our own energies — relying totally on self. But sooner or later, we find our own power insufficient. We then look toward a variety of other options — other people, money, fame, whatever. But these, too, prove insufficient. Jesus said in Matthew 28:18, "All power is given unto me in heaven and in earth." As we place our belief and trust in Jesus Christ, we then have the freedom to draw upon his power. His power is sufficient!

## Message Skit #5

# False Impressions*

**NUMBER OF MIMES:** two

**PROPS:** fancy clothing for male, cigarette, glass

**SETTING:** Mime #1 (GIRL) enters and sits down. (Can be reading, eating or whatever.) Mime #2 (BOY) enters; sees GIRL, and likes what he sees! BOY decides to make a big impression on the GIRL so she will like him.

**BOY decides his clothes are not right, so he exits and re-enters, "decked out."** *(Could be top hat, bow tie and cane, fancy sequined jacket, etc.)* **BOY walks by the GIRL, hoping she will look. Finally, after several attempts, he gets her attention. She sees him as a real weirdo, however, and tries hard to keep from laughing at him. BOY exits.**

**BOY returns** *(Without fancy clothing)***, puffing on a cigarette. He sits down behind her** *(His back to her back)***. He tries to act cool and puffs away. GIRL is annoyed by the smoke and soon begins coughing and choking. When BOY realizes what is happening, he tries to apologize, but all the GIRL wants to do is get away for some fresh air. GIRL runs out. BOY is depressed and unsure of what to do. BOY exits as GIRL re-enters. After making sure he is gone, GIRL sits back down.**

**BOY re-enters, carrying a drink in left hand.** *(It only need appear to be an alcoholic beverage.)* **He struts in, cool and arrogant. He takes a sip and chokes on it, obviously not used to strong drink. He strolls over to her. He is just about ready to speak to her when she looks**

*Performance rights for this skit are granted with the purchase of this book. No further permission is needed to adapt or integrate this skit within any performance situation for mime ministry.

up and asks him the time. Overjoyed that she spoke to him, he turns his left arm over to look at his watch, forgetting that he is holding his drink in his left hand. The drink spills onto the GIRL'S lap. She jumps up and runs out.

BOY has had it. He puts the glass down and exits.

*SCRIPTURE THOUGHT:* In Genesis, we read the story of Jacob and Esau and their father, Isaac. Jacob, disguised as his brother Esau, deceived his father and obtained his brother's birthright and blessing. We are told in the scriptures that deceit is not of the Lord, and that the deceitful man will be punished. (Psalm 5:6)

## *Message Skit #6*

# Reap What You Sow*

*NUMBER OF MIMES:* five

*PROPS:* blocks, apron, mixing bowl and spoon, attaché case and newspaper

All mimes, except MIME #1, enter and take their respective places. All freeze in position:

**2**

**1**  enters    **3**    **4**    **5**

MIME #2 unfreezes and begins pacing the floor. MIME #1 enters, knocks on his boss' *(MIME #2)* imaginary door and enters the imaginary office.

---

*Performance rights for this skit are granted with the purchase of this book. No further permission is needed to adapt or integrate this skit within any performance situation for mime ministry.

**MIME #2 angrily yells at MIME #1. MIME #1 leaves office** *(Going toward MIME #3)* **and is upset. MIME #2 exits.**

**MIME #1 arrives home, where his wife** *(MIME #3)* **lovingly greets him. MIME #1 is still so angry, though, that he yells at his wife. MIME #1 exits.**

**MIME #3** *(Wife)* **walks into next area, where MIME #4** *(Child)* **is happily playing with blocks. MIME #3 trips over a block and yells at child. MIME #3 exits.**

**MIME #4** *(Child)* **goes outside, where his dog** *(MIME #5)* **jumps on him and wants to play. MIME #4 angrily yells at his dog to stay down. MIME #4 exits.**

**MIME #2** *(Boss)* **walks by the dog on his way home from work.** *(Carries attaché case and newspaper under arm.)* **Dog** *(MIME #5)* **jumps up, barks at the boss, and sinks his teeth into the man's pant leg. Boss finally gets away and runs off. Dog exits.** *(Ad-lib for comical effect.)*

***SCRIPTURE THOUGHT:*** We should not allow our actions and attitudes to be determined by other people's words and actions. You have heard that "you will reap what you sow." There is certainly much truth in this statement.

# CHAPTER 13

# CHRISTIAN MIMES & WORKSHOPS

There are more and more Christian performers of mime today, several of whom lead workshops on mime techniques. Many teach a combination of mime and clowning because the two are so often used together in ministry.

## FLOYD SHAFFER

A Lutheran minister who was a pioneer in the area of clown ministry, Floyd Shaffer is also known as Socataco the clown. He is a master at incorporating mime into the worship experience. My first exposure to the clown as minister came from attending a conference led by a man who had been inspired by Floyd Shaffer's expression through mime. Mr. Shaffer continues to share his knowledge of and insights into clown ministry in personal appearances nationwide.

## MARK McMASTERS

One of the most outstanding Christian mime ministers today is Mark McMasters of Ashboro, North Carolina. Mark received a bachelor's degree in religion from Gardener-Webb College and then attend The Dell'Arte School of Mime and Comedy in Blue Lake, California, where he studied under Carlo Mazzone-Clementi, former partner of Marcel Marceau. Mark has ministered and performed in many churches and schools and at conferences throughout the southeastern United States. Says a brochure featuring him, "Mark ministers and entertains through a number of fun and serious illusion mime skits, as well as through sketches featuring his clown [character], Lumbo. He is able to adapt his program to the needs of the churches, schools or organizations where he is invited to perform."

# DOUGLAS BERKY

Douglas Berky is a performer and a teacher of various theatre forms and traditions. Douglas' credentials in training, performing and teaching are all exceptional. He offers workshops and lecture demonstrations in various areas, including mime, mask-making, clowning, clowning, theatre for the deaf and children's introduction to theatre.

# RANDALL BANE

Randall Bane is another pantomime artist who is an excellent performer and teacher. He directs a full-fledged ministry called

David's House, which takes him all over the United States, Canada, and western Europe. Before he began his mime ministry, he trained in New York as a method actor, performing in avant garde and experimental theatre. He later was to use dance and drama in his work in mental health therapy.

For booking information, contact Randall Bane at P.O. Box 412861, Kansas City, Missouri 64141.

## SUSIE TOOMEY

My initial plunge into the world of mime and clowning came after I attended a conference on clowning during Student Week at Ridgecrest Baptist Conference Center in Black Mountain, North Carolina, in 1976. After experiencing an entire worship service in mime, I walked from that conference room filled with excitement and anticipation of my future ministry.

I returned to the college where my husband was a campus minister, and there I organized my first clown troupe, whose total emphasis was the presentation of the gospel through mime. Since then, I have organized and directed other clown troupes. Presently, I direct "The Rainbow Connection." I continue to enjoy leading conferences and workshops on clowning and mime, and am often accompanied by the two youngest clowns in my family, Kelly and Chris.

## WORKSHOPS ON MIME

Once you have begun your journey into the world of mime, you will probably be eager to gain more knowledge and advance your skills. One way to do so is to read all the books on mime that you can. (Many are listed under Resources.) Another way is to attend workshops and conferences on mime and Christian ministry. I'm sure that there are many workshops available, but three with which I am familiar and would recommend are:

Lifeway Christian Resources
127 Ninth Avenue North
Nashville, TN 37234

Tennessee Baptist Dramatic Arts Festival
Tennessee Baptist Convention
Box 728
Brentwood, TN 37024
(800) 558-2090

Conference Opportunities for Clowns, Mimes,
Puppeteers, Dancers, and Storytellers
Phoenix Performing Arts Ministries
P.O. Box 317
West Henrietta, NY 14586

# RESOURCES

## BOOKS

Avital, Samuel. *Mime and Beyond: The Silent Outcry.* Studio City, CA: Players Press, Inc., 1985

Enters, Angna. *On Mime.* Middletown, CT: Wesleyan University Press, 1978. *This is a collection which includes anecdotes, teaching experiences, and a discussion of method.*

Fedor, Happy Jack. *Mime Time.* Colorado Springs, CO: Meriwether Publishing Ltd., 1992.

Kipnis, Claude. *The Mime Book.* Colorado Springs, CO: Meriwether Publishing Ltd., 1988.

Polsky, Milton E. *Let's Improvise: Becoming Creative, Expressive, and Spontaneous Through Drama.* New York, NY: Applause Theatre Books, 1998.

Rolfe, Bari. *Behind the Mask.* Oakland, CA: Personabooks, 1977.

Rolfe, Bari. *Commedia Dell'Arte: A Scene Study Book.* Oakland, CA: Personabooks, 1977. *A history of commedia dell'arte. Includes comic bits and scenes.*

Spolin, Viola. *Improvisations for the Theatre.* Evanston, IL: Northwestern University Press, 1983.

Straub, Cindie and Matthew. *Mime: Basics for Beginners.* Boston, MA: Plays, Inc., 1984.

## SCHOOLS/COURSES

Clown Camp
University of Wisconsin — La Crosse
Extended Education
1725 State Street
La Crosse, WI 54601

Le Centre Du Silence Mime School
Samuel Avital, Founder & Director
P.O. Box 1015 (Mimin)
Boulder, CO 80306-1015
Website: http://www.indranet.com/lcds.html

## VIDEOTAPES

From Contemporary Drama Service, Box 7710,
Colorado Springs, CO 80933

*The Art of Mime,* featuring Dr. E. Reid Gilbert and Robin Pyle

*The Mastery of Mimodrame,* featuring Todd and Marilyn Farley

*The Mastery of Mimodrame II,* featuring Todd and Marilyn Farley

*The Mastery of Mimodrame III,* featuring Todd and Marilyn Farley

*A Study in Rhythms and Concepts,* featuring Todd and Marilyn Farley

## SKITS AND PLAYS

Write for the annual catalog of Clown, Mime, Puppet, Dance, and Storytelling Resources from Contemporary Drama Service, P.O. Box 7710, Colorado Springs, CO 80933. Some sample products include:

*Clown Mimes for Christian Ministry I,* by Susie Kelly Toomey. Eight thematic clown mime skits demonstrating Christian principles.

*Clown Mimes for Christian Ministry II,* by Susie Kelly Toomey. Eight more clown mimes for outreach ministry.

*The Gospel According to Clowns,* by Mark D. Stucky. Ten skits on the life of Jesus for pantomiming clowns.

*Mime Time,* by Debbie Howell. A collection of eight secular slice-of-life mime skits.

*Pantomime Performance Exercises Workshop Kit,* by Gerald Lee Ratliff. Fourteen exercises with performance sketches

## ABOUT THE AUTHOR

Susie Toomey has chosen clowning and mime as her personal ministry. She frequently serves as a leader of weekend and week-long conferences on Christian clown and mime ministry. She has organized college students into performing troupes and she is presently directing her own clown and mime troupe, called "The Rainbow Connection."

Mrs. Toomey's husband Rick is an ordained minister who directs a counseling program for the Tennessee Eastman Co. in Kingsport, Tennessee. The couple has two children, Kelly and Chris, who have been performing as clown mimes since they were preschoolers.

The outgoing Susie Toomey is also a teacher of many years' experience at the secondary and college level. She holds both a bachelor's and a master's degree in education. Currently, she teaches and coaches a class called "Clowning and Mime in Christian Ministry."

In addition to her many clown and mime activities, she is very much involved in her own church and in denominational work.

# Order Form

**Meriwether Publishing Ltd.**
P.O. Box 7710
Colorado Springs, CO 80933
Telephone: (719) 594-4422
Website: www.meriwether publishing.com

*Please send me the following books:*

_____ **Mime Ministry  #BK-B198**                    **$12.95**
by Susie Kelly Toomey
*The first complete guidebook to Christian mime*

_____ **The Clown Ministry Handbook  #BK-B163** **$12.95**
by Janet Litherland
*The first and most complete text on the art of clown ministry*

_____ **The Mime Book  #BK-B124**                    **$14.95**
by Claude Kipnis
*A comprehensive guide to the art of mime*

_____ **Mime Time  BK B101**                          **$12.95**
by Happy Jack Feder
*A book of mime routines and performance tips*

_____ **Everything New and Who's Who in**            **$12.95**
**Clown Ministry #BK-B126**
by Janet Litherland
*Profiles of clown ministers plus 75 skits for special days*

_____ **Fool of the Kingdom  #BK-B202**              **$12.95**
by Philip D. Noble
*How to be an effective clown minister*

_____ **Clown Act Omnibus  #BK-B118**                **$14.95**
by Wes McVicar
*Everything you need to know about clowning*

These and other fine Meriwether Publishing books are available at
your local bookstore or direct from the publisher. Use the handy
order form on this page.

Name: _____

Organization name: _____

Address: _____

City: _____ State: _____

Zip: _____ Phone: _____
&#9633; **Check Enclosed**
&#9633; **Visa or MasterCard #** _____
                                        *Expiration*
*Signature:* _____ *Date:* _____
          *(required for Visa/MasterCard orders)*

**COLORADO RESIDENTS:** Please add 3% sales tax.
**SHIPPING:** Include $2.75 for the first book and 50¢ for each additional book ordered.

&#9633; *Please send me a copy of your complete catalog of books and plays.*